Manage Your Time to Reduce Your Stress

BY THE SAME AUTHOR

The Procrastinator's Handbook
The Procrastinating Child
The Clutter-Busting Handbook

Manage Your Time
to Reduce Your Stress

A HANDBOOK FOR THE OVERWORKED, OVERSCHEDULED, AND OVERWHELMED

Rita Emmett

Published by Walker Publishing Company, Inc., New York

All papers used by Walker & Company are natural, recyclable products made from wood grown in well-managed forests. The manufacturing processes conform to the environmental regulations of the country of origin.

LIBRARY OF CONGRESS CATALOGING-IN-PUBLICATION DATA

Emmett, Rita.
Manage your time to reduce your stress : a handbook for the overworked, overscheduled, and overwhelmed / Rita Emmett. —1st U.S. ed.
p.   cm.
Includes bibliographical references and index.
ISBN-13: 978-0-8027-1648-4 (alk. paper)
ISBN-10: 0-8027-1648-2 (alk. paper)
1. Time management.   2. Stress management.   I. Title.
BF637.T5E46   2009
640'.43—dc22
2008022110

Visit Walker & Company's Web site at www.walkerbooks.com

First U.S. edition 2009

1   3   5   7   9   10   8   6   4   2

Designed by Rachel Reiss
Typeset by Westchester Book Group
Printed in the United States of America by Quebecor World Fairfield

*This book is dedicated to all you wonderful,
intelligent, hardworking people who want to add a
richer, more peaceful and relaxed quality to your life
and care enough about it to actually read this book.
Here's wishing you times of love and laughter,
the blessings of health and wealth,
the joy of family and friends,
and many restful, re-creating moments of serenity.*

Author's Note

To protect the privacy of my readers and seminar participants who have given permission for their stories to appear in this book, their names and identifying characteristics have been changed, with the exception of those professionals who have provided comments and have given permission for their names to be published.

Contents

Acknowledgments and Appreciation   xi

Introduction   3

1. It's Time to Get Control of That Stress   7

2. Search for and Select What Is Valuable in Your Life   28

3. Trash Perfectionism   49

4. Reach for Realistic Goals That Are Both Relevant
   and Rewarding   67

5. Eliminate What You Can and Streamline
   Everything Else   90

6. Set Boundaries at Work and at Home   115

7. Strive to Recharge Your Battery Daily   137

8. Now Let's Put It All Together   157

Index   183

Acknowledgments and Appreciation

Writing a book and having it published is a dream come true, a blessing from God, a huge hunk of the luck of the Irish, and—no matter what you call it—it's a blast.

The author gets all the praise and honor (also criticism and bad reviews, but that's another story), but this book wouldn't be in your hands if it weren't for a glorious gang offering help, support, and encouragement on both the professional and personal levels.

My deepest gratitude goes to the three—editor, agent, and publisher—who helped turn my random, chaotic thoughts into a readable book and who have guided me through the writing and publishing of my three previous books as well as this one. Thank you to:

Jackie Johnson, who I am convinced is not only one of the world's finest editors, but also one of the world's most patient people. She works hard to polish my words, so if there is a shine or a sparkle to this book, we have Jackie to thank for it. She guides and answers, coaches and coaxes, and never makes fun of my disorganized way of thinking . . . and writing.

Danielle Egan-Miller, my fabulous literary agent, who listens patiently, works tirelessly, treats me as if she has all the time in the world for me, and turns my weird ideas into something that can be published—all with a delightful sense of humor and a wealth of wisdom.

George Gibson, publisher, who, while surrounded at Walker & Company by so many authors who are scholars and researchers, continues to welcome, support, and promote my books.

It's a delight and honor to be associated with all three as well as the whole team at Walker & Company who have enriched my life and worked hard to turn this book into a reality.

An enormous thank-you to so many others, including Mickey Forster, my niece, Web goddess, friend, assistant, and general guiding light. I don't know what I would have done without her fun and loving help.

She and the rest of my Dream Team, Cheryl Guidry, Brian Redding, and Stormi Willis, have played a vital role in supporting and encouraging this book and providing ways for Emmett Enterprises, Inc., to help people break the procrastination and clutter habits.

A heartfelt thanks to Randy Davis for mentoring, teaching, coaching, and guiding me to new ways of thinking; for pushing me off the edge so I can fly; for wisdom, humor, and caring; and most of all for his friendship.

Tremendous gratitude to all my family and friends who cheered me on, helped in any way they could, and put up with my absentmindedness and lack of availability when I was writing, and special thanks to those of you who offered your enthusiasm and stories or were willing to read and offer guidance on this book, especially Michelle Emmett, Ruth Coleman, Jessa Forster, Carolyn (CJ) Jonasen, Tomas Dorney, JoAnne Knight, Linda Brakeall, and Curt Hansen, all of whom offered constant friendship and support. Also thank you for help and stories: Malachy McCourt, Kay Merkle, Sandra Baumgardner, Phaedra Vaughan, and Norma Maloney.

There's always a special hug and smooch for my long-suffering husband, Bruce, who did such a brilliant job at picking up the slack and keeping our lives on an even keel while I was cloistered in my "cell where I dwell" writing this book.

Thank you to all of you (and I do apologize if I accidentally left out your name). And most of all, my deepest gratitude to clients, subscribers to our Tip Sheet electronic newsletter, and readers of my books, including you.

Thank you for reading this book and thank you, God, for this joyful journey.

Manage Your Time to Reduce Your Stress

Introduction

TWENTY YEARS AGO, WHEN I FIRST started presenting "Blast Away Procrastination" seminars, I observed that people put off things they hate to do. These days, people still put off what they hate to do, but—to me—the biggest change in that area is that they also put off what they *love* to do.

Over and over I hear of how people used to see their friends every week, but now their life is so busy that visits occur only a few times a year. Or how they love to read novels, but they have so many other things they have to read, there is never time for "reading the books I love." Or the whole family used to gather for dinner every weekend, but now they come together only on holidays. Or they tell of how much they love going to the movies or plays, walking in nature, visiting museums, entertaining, playing the tuba, working out, building models, sewing, and all sorts of activities that nurture their spirits and recharge their batteries, but . . . well, you know how it goes: so much to do and so little time.

People are busy building the lives they *thought* they wanted; they have become so stressed out that they have no life.

Are you putting off the life you want to enjoy? Regardless of how productive, effective, and efficient you may be, if you answer yes to one of the following questions, you are procrastinating.

Do you put off learning ways to manage your stress until the busy time ends?

Do you put off spending time with people you love until you're less busy?

Are you waiting for a busy time to end before you take steps to improve your life? *Manage Your Time to Reduce Your Stress* will address a very common problem shared by many: the feeling that the more productive you become, the more there is to do, and there just isn't any time or energy left to do those enjoyable things you really want to do.

Where would you find the time?

No one really *finds* time. Imagine walking along and stumbling across a big ol' bucket of extra time. It just doesn't happen. You have to *make* time, and this book will help you figure out how to make time (guilt-free) and use it in areas of your life that you value.

People who have read my previous books or attended my seminars tell me that they are successful in breaking the procrastination and clutter habits, but they are still outrageously stressed and have more responsibilities than they can handle. They know they need to nurture their health, but they keep putting it off because there are so many more important things to do. They are overworked, overscheduled, and overwhelmed. And what makes matters worse is they are concerned that if they start to use stress management concepts, all of their time management techniques will suffer because they will have to sit under a tree smelling the roses, accomplishing nothing and never drinking caffeine again.

Manage Your Time to Reduce Your Stress: A Handbook for the Overworked, Overscheduled, and Overwhelmed will tackle time management *not* in terms of becoming more productive or efficient, but in terms of how we spend our time in relation to all that is important and valuable to us in our lives, and how to continue to be productive and efficient without burning out.

Life isn't time management, it is "stuff" management—things to do, people to see, commitments and obligations to fulfill. And *mis*managing all that stuff-to-do is what leads to stress and feeling fragmented, frantic, frazzled, and frustrated.

This book will address stress *not* in terms of nutrition, exercise, what you drink, or whether you smoke, but will focus on the impact time management has on stress, what you can and cannot control about it, and how to make changes in your time management that will have an enormous impact on alleviating your stress. In addition, this book will help you:

- Understand that learning to manage your stress can be one of the finest gifts you ever give yourself
- Acknowledge that eliminating all stress is not the solution
- Unearth ways to add fun to your life
- Reassess that guilty feeling that might pop up when you do something to add fun to your life
- Understand why it is crucial to stop being a perfectionist (and how to do that)
- Find ways to simplify your life
- Move from fatigue to energy

At the end of each chapter, there is an Extra Credit section of questions and exercises prompting you to record insights, lessons learned, and decisions. You can skip this section, but doing these exercises will deepen your experience and understanding of how to manage your time to lessen your stress. Also make note of the places in this book that discuss areas you want to work on. You'll read some ideas that point out the good things you're already doing and other areas that you need to work on. You will identify your strengths and your weaknesses.

Highlight strategies you believe may work for you, then put them into practice. If one doesn't work, try another until you have your own personalized plan. If you find yourself backsliding and feeling close to burnout, you can review any section that applies to you. Use this book as a reference that you can refer to over and over. It will change your life.

CHAPTER 1

It's Time to Get
Control of That Stress

JULIE TOOK GREAT PRIDE IN BEING a super-achiever in a waste management company; she loved a sense of accomplishment and success. But she felt that there was an emptiness inside her. She had way too much to do and never enough time to do it. As a result she didn't have time for the people she loved, and when she was asked if she ever had fun, she laughed, shrugged her shoulders, and replied, "When would I have time for fun?" But Julie assured everyone that she loved her work. Even though she was working with people all day long, Julie was lonely. She was always tired and took medication for depression and anxiety.

Dennis is a financial adviser who constantly races from meeting to meeting. He handles a huge list of phone calls as he drives from place to place and says he loves his fast-paced life. Yet he has no life except his work. His family has drifted away from him and he has no friends. He's a likable guy and many people would love to spend time with him, but he's always too busy to socialize. He too says he loves his work.

Family members express concern over his health but he says the stress doesn't bother him. He does plan to start an exercise program to lose the weight around his middle, and he knows that if he eats in a more healthy way he will feel better. But there just isn't time. Also, he has insomnia—he wakes up around 2:00 A.M. and stays awake. As a result, he is exhausted most of the time.

He says others might need self-care, but he doesn't. His blood pressure is out of control, he is on medication for cholesterol and several other challenges, and he is always in a frantic, frazzled state. What Dennis doesn't realize is that those who say they don't need downtime, quiet time, or time for themselves are often the ones who need it the most.

Shay and Marcie are partners in their own network marketing business, which they run out of their home. They love what they do but have no boundaries. So they accept phone calls during family time and drop their work to take care of the kids, but then feel that they have to make up that time by working late into the night. On weekends, if a business crisis comes up or a deadline looms, they put aside time with the children to work in the office, and they often feel guilty about canceled family plans, so they make up for it by buying the latest toy or techno-gadget for the children.

As a consequence, they are deeply in debt, which makes them decide to spend more time working to catch up financially, which leaves them feeling guilty for ignoring the kids, so they buy more and more stuff for them. This vicious circle has contributed to arguments, sleep deprivation, overweight for both Shay and Marcie, and short tempers on everyone's part.

Some people are so caught up in being productive, efficient, and stressed-out that they accept burnout as a normal way of life. They think the concept of enjoying life is airy-fairy New Age baloney.

In a seminar, Stan said he was tired of being swamped by all that he had to do and the busy-ness of his life. He felt he was under so much stress and there were so many demands being made on his time each day that stress management couldn't possibly work for him.

On the other hand, he wondered about several people he knew—including his boss—who experienced enormous demands on their time but were able to get an amazing amount of work done and meet an awesome amount of deadlines, yet remained calm and had time for family and friends. So he decided to learn about stress management, trusting that he too could find a way to avoid burnout in the midst of his super-busy life.

As we work to be more productive and accomplish more and more, many of us are hyper-scheduled—so busy that there is no time to:

Sleep late—ever—or read the Sunday newspaper or magazines

Make love or cuddle

Recharge batteries or refresh your soul

Go to the zoo, museum, botanical garden, movies, theater, or concerts

Clutter-bust desks, e-mails, cars, or homes

Garden or pursue other hobbies

Create a home that feels like a sanctuary of comfort and rest

Help a neighbor or work for a favorite worthy cause

Loaf or think or pray or relax or journal or meditate or . . . rest

Think . . . or feel . . . or enjoy life

Ask yourself what the purpose of your busy-ness is. Does it bring you contentment or joy? Some people overschedule themselves or take on more work and responsibilities than they can handle reasonably because they are highly competitive and want to be perceived as the best or most powerful or strongest or most successful at whatever they do. Some overextend themselves out of a desire for the love and approval of others.

Fear also can be motivation, especially in a highly competitive job market where those who have jobs must work hard to keep them, sometimes increasing their workload to absorb the duties of laid-off colleagues.

How will you know when you achieve success? Do you know what you are striving for? Is it the right success for you? Are you working to make enough money? But how much is enough? When will you know you've got enough?

We become accustomed to stress, so used to it that in spite of the frenetic pace, multiple top priorities, and high demands of everyday life in the twenty-first century, it seems that managing stress has become a low priority for many people.

What Stress Really Is

Dr. Jamie Kahon, a chiropractor in Illinois, explains that in stressful situations—whether the stress hits you physically, intellectually, emotionally, or spiritually—your body releases a hormone called cortisol. It is produced by the adrenal glands, which lie on top of the kidneys, and it helps you to adapt to stressful situations.

Cortisol, often referred to as the "stress hormone," is intricately involved in many physiological functions, including the regulation of healthy blood sugar metabolism, maintenance of healthy blood pressure levels, establishment of healthy immune system function, and promotion of the body's natural anti-inflammatory response.

But when exposed to excessive demands, the brain sends a message to the adrenal glands to increase cortisol secretion. The body responds by providing a surge in energy, increasing mental alertness, and raising blood pressure, thereby preparing the body for the "fight or flight" response.

While this response provides an effective mechanism for combating an acute stressor, increased or prolonged exposure to stress can lead to elevated cortisol levels. And heightened cortisol, in turn, can lead to negative changes in body chemistry, altering the balance of hormones and affecting the systems of the body.

As cortisol increases, it can reach a level where it becomes life-threatening as it increases the body's secretion of insulin, which can cause insulin resistance, metabolic syndrome, infertility, etc. This can lead to diabetes, which can cause heart disease, kidney failure, tingling in the hands and feet, blindness, and even amputation of limbs, among a host of other complications.

When illness hits you, it can touch you on the physical, intellectual, emotional, or spiritual level. Physical symptoms might be headaches or stomach problems; intellectual symptoms might be absentmindedness or indecisiveness; emotional symptoms might be out of control anger or weeping. Even people who aren't religious recognize that we all have a spiritual part to ourselves, and spiritual stress can manifest in that feeling of emptiness or the feeling that we have nothing left to give. Burnout.

There are many different concepts of what stress is. For example, one definition of stress is the result of trying to do too much, for too many people, in too little time, in an environment that is too hard to deal with. When you let go of trying to control an inflexible environment and all the people in it, you stop struggling with fantasy and the pain of unrealistic expectations. You let go of stress.

We can all relate to this, but let's turn to Dr. Hans Selye, the Canadian endocrinologist and father of stress research. His definition is the one I use in my seminars. He writes, "Stress is the nonspecific response of the body to any demand made upon it."

The secret of stress management is grasping the concept that we have zero control over the stressors or demands made upon us, yet we have 100 percent control over our response. That's where the management of stress must start.

The demands/stressors in your life are neither good nor bad. It is only our reaction or response that turns us into raving lunatics. And we could have a negative stress response to negative *or* positive demands. Getting married or divorced, hired or fired, graduating or dropping out of school—all are demands upon us.

For example, vacations are supposed to be fun, positive. Have you ever taken a road trip for three days with kids in the backseat? See what I mean? Vacations are *supposed* to be positive. But many times, people are outrageously stressed by vacations or other positive demands such as holidays or weddings.

Why We Experience Burnout

Technology and labor-saving devices are time savers, but using them may not lead to us getting more rest or relaxation. What are we doing with all the extra time we have that has been saved for us by dishwashers, cell phones, e-mail, computers, and all our time-saving appliances?

We have more choices, but we also have more expectations, noise, complications, anxiety, and depression. We have more loneliness than ever before, and have more worries about jobs, debt, family, finances, insecurity at work, and the future of the world.

Carolyn, a participant in my time-management seminar, had an interesting insight. She said she often receives e-mails with articles by people longing for "the good ol' days." "But remember," she wrote in her blog, "the good ol' days were kind of rough to live through—there were no televisions, no phones, no cars, no indoor plumbing, no electricity, no air-conditioning, no deodorant, no computers; so many luxuries that we take for granted weren't available."

Carolyn is right. The good ol' days were not a great time for minorities, widows, orphans, or the poor; there was little assistance or advocacy for the elderly or children, the mentally ill or disabled, or for people who were battered, shattered, scared, abused, or confused.

Yes, people lived slower lives, but that doesn't mean they were free of stress. Jake's grandfather told of working on the farm from sunup until sundown when a hailstorm wiped out all of his crops. His grandfather said, "There was no insurance when that happened and also no miracles of modern medicine to cure illnesses or save lives." Just those two examples alone must have caused great worry, concern, and, yes, stress.

Ida, a woman in her late eighties, told me that her three young brothers all died the same week of the same illness, and she said that was not uncommon. She said the heartbreak from that almost killed her mother.

As long as people have lived, there have been stressful situations of one degree or another. Let's not wish for the peace and stress-free serenity of the good ol' days. That is a fantasy. But the reality is, we can improve our lives right now regardless of the demands being made upon us.

We have a different stress, that's all. Never has there been such a combination of pressures such as:

- living on the edge
- being available to work every minute of the day with cell phones, e-mail, text messages, PDAs, and all the other "helpful technology" coming our way
- constantly rushing at a fast pace
- trying to multitask with two, three, or four activities demanding our attention at the same time
- overcommitting ourselves

- needing medication for going to sleep, waking up, and staying alert or energized
- fear of losing a job
- being sandwiched between needy aging parents and needy adult kids
- complications
- lack of boundaries
- insecurity
- fear
- lack of fulfilling relationships
- complete exhaustion

Burnout is often called the illness of the very caring. Someone who doesn't give a dang about other people or the world isn't as prone to burnout as you are.

Obviously, you are out there living life and caring. Does that mean you *will* burn out? No. But it does mean that you could be prone to it, so you must be aware of the high price you could pay for stress and need to learn positive ways to prevent it . . . such as reading this book.

When you manage your stress in negative or unhealthy ways, the outcome often is sickness. For example, high blood pressure and heart disease can be caused by stress. And there are many illnesses and conditions such as asthma that are not caused by stress but can be exacerbated by it.

STRESS: COPING STRATEGIES

UNHEALTHY	HEALTHY
Smoking	Exercising
Drinking alcohol	Relaxing
Overeating	Practicing good nutrition
Using drugs	Doing recreational activities
Withdrawing	Being assertive
Indulging in self-pity	Taking time-outs
Blaming	Using humor

One sign of burnout is when someone (maybe you?) says phrases such as "I just don't care," "I hate it here," "I can't take this anymore," "Every day I wish I could quit my job," and "Stay away from me. Leave me alone."

What is the solution? Should we strive for a life free of all stress? Nope, not possible and not desirable. No matter what your life circumstance, there will be stress. A life without stress would mean there's no reason to get out of bed in the morning. As glorious as that may sound, life would get pretty boring in no time, and guess what? Boredom, for most people, is more stressful than rush-hour traffic in New York.

The secret is to learn to manage stress in positive ways. One of the best gifts you can ever give yourself is to become an expert in stress management.

How to Control Your Responses to Stressors

Daniel, a cable guy, told a story that was a great example of several people having widely different responses to the exact same demand. He had been stuck for fifteen minutes waiting for a train to pass. The train finally ended, two cars ahead of him crossed the tracks, and then he had to wait for another train coming from the opposite direction to pass.

He started to feel his heart pounding in his head because he was late for an important appointment. To distract himself from feeling frantic, he decided to observe people in the cars around him.

A few cars behind him, a guy was in major meltdown, pounding his horn and swearing out the window at the top of his lungs. Daniel wondered what his purpose could possibly be. Did the guy think the railroad engineer would hear him, stop the train, and say, "Oh my, my, my. Please excuse me, am I inconveniencing you? Allow me to back up and clear this track for you."

The woman next to him reached into her glove box, pulled out a large plastic bag filled with postcards, stamps, and a pen, and sat calmly writing notes to people. Daniel said, "Now there's a woman who has a train-waiting strategy."

The fellow in front of him fell sound asleep at the wheel and when the train finally ended, Daniel had to beep to wake him up.

Our level of stress has nothing to do with the demands made upon us and has everything to do with our response. It's up to us to control our responses; our feelings contribute to our responses, but our thoughts generate those feelings. What we say to ourselves (our self-talk) determines those thoughts. Sound hard? It's really not, and the rest of this book will help you develop new attitudes and new ways of talking to yourself.

In Daniel's instance, we saw examples of a whole range of self-talk. The fellow frantically beeping and yelling probably told himself that this was the worst thing that could happen to him at that moment and his whole life would be ruined if that train didn't end right then. Isn't that a common message that teens give their parents? "If you don't let me go out tonight, my whole life will be ruined."

The other two drivers could have had the same time crunch as yelling-beeper guy and could have had the same amount of pressure on them, but they told themselves that no matter how frazzled or frustrated they got, it was not going to get them across those train tracks any faster. So they might as well make the best of it. (And maybe leave a little earlier next time.)

These messages of self-talk have great power over our mental and physical health. Yelling-beeper guy's blood pressure reading probably would have been soaring at that moment.

Another example of how self-talk can overcome stress would be if your absentminded neighbor always forgets to tell his wife you called and want her to call you back; your self-talk would be more important than his lack of communication. If you tell yourself he is rude and inconsiderate and you deserve to be treated better, you can work yourself into a frenzy. On the other hand, if you tell yourself, "Well, I left a message but I know he never remembers to tell her. So I'll just pretend I didn't make the call and I'll try to reach her later," that self-talk will likely reduce your stress response.

Great Questions to Ask Yourself Frequently

Examine your existing concept of time management in order to recognize when doing more is actually taking time away from what you really *want* to do. Some of the questions we all need to ask ourselves occasionally include:

1. Do I work excessive hours because I'm passionate about my work or because I'm scared not to?
2. Right now, is my work exhausting or exhilarating?
3. Do I have some source of joy in my life?

If that last question sounds naive and simplistic to you, then you desperately need this book. It is not normal and should not be acceptable to you to live with no expectation of happiness or joy.

Our lives are like bank accounts. You need to make deposits in the form of doing things to care for yourself physically, intellectually, emotionally, and spiritually. If you keep making withdrawals for work and other commitments without making a deposit, you'll burn out. If you went to the doctor and she told you that you will die if you don't slow down and take care of yourself, you would make the time. Why wait till the doctor tells you to take care of yourself? Why not prevent that doctor visit from happening?

Burnout often happens when your stress, work, or frustration is greater than the reward, success, or appreciation you receive. Have you ever had an experience where you worked hard and got a thank-you and a great pat on the back, and you said, "I'll do it again. I'll work for that person [or organization] any time they want me to." For most people, a little appreciation goes a long way. And the opposite is true, too. Lack of appreciation usually leads to cranky people.

Burnout is not limited to white-collar professionals. Anyone can suffer burnout on many levels, such as an adult son or daughter caring for an aging (or ill, or simply mean) parent. You could burn out when you need a break from your kids, a spouse, a volunteer organization, needy friends, clutter, work, or drudgery.

Sinking a Float

For example, Sylvia, a graphic designer, was in charge of building a rainbow float to represent the school PTA in her town's Independence Day parade. She formed a huge rainbow out of chicken wire, and then thousands of paper napkins were fluffed open and stuffed into each and every hole.

Many people offered to help fluff and stuff, but truly it was Sylvia's project, and it took her every waking moment for over a month. But Sylvia kept telling everyone it was worth the time and effort, because the float would be used several times later. After the parade, it would be stored in a PTA member's storehouse to be used again for the harvest parade, the Brownie fly-up ceremony, and the Christmas pageant.

When the July parade ended, Sylvia went to the PTA president to let her know she was going to deliver the float to the storehouse and was shocked to hear that there no longer was room for the float in there. Sylvia asked what she should do and was told that she should dump the float in the garbage.

She did.

But she was burned out from too much work and too little appreciation. She never volunteered for that PTA again. But every year she is the arts and crafts lady for the local church "Summer Happening." At the end of summer, the group gives her a thank-you mug, a certificate, and applause. None of these cost much time or money, but they made Sylvia feel appreciated and that's all the reward she needs.

Most of us don't work in a place or live in a world that has a system for rewards or appreciation. So guess where I think the reward or appreciation has to come from? Not from the boss— when they go to "Boss School" they learn delegation, leadership, and how to spell "priorities," but not how to show appreciation.

So who's in charge of making you feel appreciated and rewarding you? That's right. You are. It's up to you to give yourself a reward: "I just finished a big project at work, and I'm going to loaf this Sunday afternoon."

Tip: It's important to communicate these plans to your family. Otherwise you'll have the whole gang circling you like buzzards asking, "Why is she relaxing when we need her to go to the store?"

QUESTIONS TO CONTEMPLATE

If you could wave a magic wand and change your stressful situations, what areas of your life would you change?

Would you connect with people more often? Or less often?

Would you stop feeling lonely?

Would you stop spending time with people who make you feel miserable?

Would you have more (or less) social activities? Group meetings? Business engagements?

Would you spend time out in nature more? Have more quiet time or meaningful time in your life?

Would you stop feeling guilty, worried, or anxious as often as you do now?

Would you stop wishing that someone or something would change so that you could finally feel happy?

Would you start to have fun?

Would you stop finding excuses to put off "recharging your battery"?

Would you have more control over your schedule? Be less hurried and harried?

Would you stop allowing impossible standards to make you crazy, standards such as perfection or never making a mistake?

Would you be more positive? Pleasant to be with? Less critical? Less judgmental?

Would you be more active? More energetic? More organized? More dependable?

Would you finally let go of your overwhelming stress?

Would you enjoy your life more?

How would your life be different?

After you give thought to these questions, here's one more: What is keeping you from spending your time on what is valuable to you?

Obviously, we don't have control over everything. You don't have much control of your time if you are caring for someone not able to care for himself, but that must not completely stop you from enjoying life, adding fun to your life, eating healthier, or whatever other changes you desire. Maybe chasing after several preschoolers all day does mean that their needs come first, and maybe working a high-pressure job does mean you don't have much time for yourself, but isn't there some way to sneak in a few minutes to take care of you?

It might take some creative problem-solving but often there is some way to squeeze little kindnesses to yourself into your daily schedule.

Final questions: Do you make everybody else more important than you are? Do you allow everybody else's needs and priorities to come before yours?

Hmmmm, these are questions worth pondering, aren't they? If you wish that someone would reduce your stress, let *you* become that someone, and start down the glorious road of experiencing the joys, rewards, and improved lifestyle that come when you give yourself the gift of stress management.

Take Care of You

With the fast pace and high demands of everyday life in the twenty-first century, it seems the pressures associated with accomplishing more impact almost everyone and anyone, from soccer moms to great-grandmothers, from college grads to retirees. Keep in mind the classic example of airplane oxygen masks. The flight attendant announces that in case of emergency the oxygen mask will drop down. The attendant also warns that if you're on a plane with someone who is not able to care for himself, you should put your oxygen mask on first. If you try to put it on the other person first, you might pass out and be totally useless to help the person who depends on you.

The same is true with self-care. Take care of you first, otherwise you might burn out and not be any good to those you care for.

During a seminar, Edwardo, a civil engineer, argued, "But wait! You think we should be responsible for our response to demands and for giving ourselves appreciation. Isn't that just adding to our responsibilities? Adding to our stress?"

I told him no, not at all. As you start to take charge of your self-talk to control your response to the demands that are bombarding you, you will see your stress start to melt away and your view of the world change.

Time management is not the only solution if you find yourself running like a hamster in a wheel, rushing to get too much done in too little time. In fact, if you are that busy, trying to do too many things *is* causing you stress. There is hidden, surprising pain in efficiency and productivity for its own sake—depression, broken relationships, financial difficulties, health problems, over-whelming schedules, and exhaustion all come under the general headings of stress and burnout.

As you start to give yourself some appreciation, rewards, and self-care, you will be amazed to find new zest, enthusiasm, and energy. With a little thought—and a few changes—you can learn how to continue to work in an efficient, productive manner without generating harmful stress and still make the time to engage in the activities you truly enjoy. This book will show you how to reach that balance.

The first letter of the next six chapters spell the word STRESS:

Search for and select what is valuable in your life

Trash perfectionism

Reach for realistic goals that are both relevant and rewarding

Eliminate what you can and streamline everything else

Set boundaries at work and at home

Strive to recharge your battery daily

The questions to begin with are: Do you know what activities you enjoy? Do you know what is important or of value in your life? Many people don't. This is what we tackle next.

Thoughts to Ponder

Stress is the spice of life. Without stress, life lacks excitement, challenge, and a sense of adventure.

—Hans Selye

No man need stay the way he is.

—Harry Emerson Fosdick

Two men look out through the same bars:
One sees the mud, and one the stars.

—Frederick Langbridge

When you complain, all you do is broadcast, "There's a victim in the neighborhood."

—Maya Angelou

Slow down and enjoy life. It's not only the scenery you miss by going too fast—you also miss the sense of where you are going and why.

—EDDIE CANTOR

Stress is an ignorant state. It believes that everything is an emergency.

—NATALIE GOLDBERG

We either make ourselves miserable or make ourselves strong, either way, the amount of work is the same.

—CARLOS CASTANEDA

Expecting the world to treat you fairly because you are good is like expecting the bull not to charge because you are a vegetarian.

—DENNIS WHOLEY

EXTRA CREDIT

1. What areas of your life cause the most challenge, difficulty, or stress for you? Identify those areas. Some ideas:
    work
    home
    relationships
    volunteer groups
    financial obligations
    schedules

sleep
health
emotions

2. How does stress hit you?
    Physically:
    Intellectually:
    Emotionally:
    Spiritually:

3. What is your biggest cause of stress?

    _____

    _____

4. What is your best way to manage stress? (What do you do to
   help yourself when you become stressed out?)

    _____

    _____

5. Occasionally ask yourself:
    a) Do I work excessive hours because I'm passionate about
       my work or because I'm scared not to?
    b) Right now, is my work exhausting or exhilarating?
    c) Do I have some source of joy in my life?
    d) Am I trying to control something that is beyond my
       control?

CHAPTER 2

Search for and Select What Is Valuable in Your Life

JOSH, A REAL ESTATE BROKER, TRULY enjoyed his career and never minded working twelve, fourteen, or sixteen hours per day. However, he battled Crohn's disease and his doctor constantly urged him to reduce the stress in his life. He didn't feel he was under stress because he enjoyed his work. But as he started experiencing more flare-ups with his disease, the doctor strongly pushed Josh to seek counseling, and he even set up the first appointment. So simply to appease the doctor, Josh decided he would go to one session.

The therapist asked him what was important in his life and he said his work. When encouraged to add anything else to the list, he quickly added, "Of course my wife and kids, and my parents and the rest of my family. Oh yeah, and my health, and the Chicago Cubs."

"What about money?"

Josh replied, "Yes, money is super important, too, and especially all the stuff money buys. Love it."

Then the therapist asked, "What on that list would you miss

the most if you lost it?" Josh thought a minute and told him, "My kids and wife, then maybe my health."

"Where do your job and money fit in?"

Josh was surprised to hear himself say, "They come after the others. I would be sad to lose my job or money, but I'd be devastated if I lost my kids or wife, and I don't want my Crohn's disease to get any worse. I want to become healthy again."

The therapist paused, then recapped: "You value your family and your health most, after that comes your career and money and all that money buys.

"So let's take a look at your life. How much time do you spend with your family, on your health . . . and with your work?"

Josh felt as if he'd been kicked in the gut.

"I spend all my time working," he said. "My wife says she feels like a single mom raising our kids. They are usually in bed by the time I get home. And over the weekend, I'm either on the phone or the computer or my BlackBerry. All my time is spent on my career and hardly any on the things that are really valuable to me."

The therapist leaned forward, his eyes riveted on Josh's, and said, "When the way you live is not in sync with your values, the result is always stress, which can lead to dis-ease."

When you spend more time doing what is not important to you, and little or no time on what is truly important to you, the result is usually stress, frustration, and a sense of inadequacy. Eventually, you have an empty feeling, as if there is not a drop of energy or joy left inside you.

Some people work progressively longer hours, their personal lives becoming emptier; then in order to avoid the emptiness, they find it easier to just keep working. You might be super busy, yet where are the relationships, the joy, and the fun you would like in life? How is it that we all get the same number of hours each day, yet how you're spending your time feels so unsatisfying?

The True Meaning of Time Management

How do you spend your time? Time management doesn't mean running around like a nut doing twenty things at once. True time management means actually spending as much of your time as you can doing those things you want to do rather than activities you don't care about. It involves clarifying your values, deciding what is important, and working to spend your time doing that.

For example, a person who highly values financial security yet devotes a great deal of time to shopping and running up debts will usually find herself stressed, joyless, and sometimes sick. Once you clarify and identify your values, then you can brainstorm ways to adhere to them.

For Josh, this meant becoming more conscious of the time he spends with his family and what he would allow to interrupt it. He has made some changes. Now when he's home he screens his calls, taking only the absolutely necessary ones. And he checks his e-mail once a day over weekends and responds only to those needing immediate attention. Most of all, he makes an effort to be present when he is with his family instead of letting his mind focus on his business during family time. As a result, his family life is happier, and he feels much closer to his wife and kids. They in turn are delighted to "have more of Daddy" and there is less stress in the whole house, which has had a positive impact on Josh's stress at work.

What our values are and how we spend our time regarding those values usually happens at an unconscious level, so it's often mystifying why you are so frazzled. To bring your values from your unconscious to your conscious mind, read this list of values and see which of them strike you as important in your life.

SOME OF THE THINGS PEOPLE VALUE

health	looks
family	beauty
friends	acceptance
money	praise
time	reward
a home	acknowledgment
education	validation
travel	nature
heirlooms	environment
photographs	Mother Earth
heritage	animals
culture	pets
religion	sports
political beliefs	TV
peace	music
power	art
adventure	science
energy	downtime
vitality	alone time
party time	compromise

winning	right to vote
control	freedom
being right	renewable energy
being popular	a promise
chocolate chip cookies	truth
food	volunteering
shelter	helping others
alcohol	pleasing others
drugs	being liked
cigarettes	success
survival	jewelry
happiness	furs
spirituality	cars
communication	motorcycles

Making time to do the things you love will reduce your stress. Are you willing to devote time to uncovering what is important to you and figuring out ways to incorporate that into your life? This is a necessary step to prevent your time management from draining you.

When people do not give some thought to their values, all their goal-setting, multitasking, and organizational strategies can lead them straight into feeling overwhelmed, which leads to burnout. And if you live your life in the fast lane, accomplishing huge numbers of projects, tasks, and goals, yet none of these brings you joy or gives you a sense of purpose, then frustration and stress will build up. You might work hard to get more done in less time, but is there any time left for experiencing fun in life? The satisfaction of a job well done? The close friendships and connections with people who nourish and enrich your spirit? The peace and serenity at the end of the day that brings soothing rest?

Do You Procrastinate About You?

Do you make time for yourself to recharge your battery, or are you too busy taking care of everyone else? People can have all the time management skills in the world, but if they believe that everyone else's priorities come first, then they will manage their time to care for everyone else, ignore themselves, be unproductive, and eventually burn out.

Why is everyone else more important than you are? Why are everyone else's priorities more important than yours?

When I first started talking in my keynote presentations and training sessions about making time for yourself and what is important to you, a woman in the audience told me that was being selfish. She said that she was raised with the Bible telling her to love her neighbor and she wondered if I was contradicting that.

I reminded her that the Bible says, "Love your neighbor as yourself." That part that says "as yourself" tends to be left off by lots of people. When you think about it, we are called to love ourselves with a good, healthy, positive love, and *then* we can love our neighbors in the same way.

Many of us reverse that—we offer much more kindness to our neighbors, friends, and family (even strangers) than we do to ourselves. One common example is the way people handle compliments. Have you ever heard someone receive a compliment such as "Nice blouse" and instead of saying "thank you" she sputters things like: "Oh, this old rag? It's been hanging in my closet for eight years. I got it at a half-price sale."

Do *you* blow off compliments that way? When we do that we're treating ourselves much more poorly than we would ever treat others. Could you imagine yourself saying the same thing to others that you say to yourself? Would you consider greeting a friend with "Hi, Mary, I see you're wearing that old rag again. Isn't that the one that's been hanging in your closet for eight years? The one you got at the half-price sale?" Of course you wouldn't. That would be stupid and rude, yet we put ourselves down in that way all the time.

To avoid burnout, you have to start with being a little kinder to yourself and treating yourself with good, healthy, positive self-love. You have to put the oxygen mask on you first—or you won't be able to help anyone.

Somehow, some way, you have to first figure out what is important to you. What are your values in life? Then you have to decide what you're willing to do to include those values in your life.

You don't want to eventually end up getting sick and hearing a doctor tell you that now you *have* to do something to take care of you.

You have to be extra vigilant if you have the type of job that makes extreme demands on you, such as:

- being available 24/7
- having a heavy travel schedule
- being physically at the workplace ten hours a day or more
- having responsibility for a large number of direct reports

- having an unpredictable flow of work
- handling a huge amount of responsibility
- having many deadlines
- being responsible for training and mentoring over and above your regular responsibilities
- being expected to attend frequent events outside regular work hours

When expectations and responsibilities at work are excessive and you can't do anything about it, then you need to make serious adjustments in your personal life.

Sometimes it takes creative problem-solving to find ways to add enjoyment to your life. Mario, a security guard, loved to sing in a chorus in high school, but after graduation, his job and working on his fixer-upper house took up all his time. Although he loved his life, one day he realized he was bored. He couldn't afford to change jobs, so he decided to search for a way to add some joy to his life outside of work.

Mario looked around for a chorus to join and discovered the answer was right in front of him—every Sunday morning. He joined his church choir and once again is delighted to be part of the glorious harmonies of a singing group. He says his choir has lifted his spirits and given him a new zest for life.

The word "recreation" breaks down to "re-create." Do you have any form of recreation in your life which leaves you feeling "re-created" physically, mentally, emotionally, or spiritually?

Seventeen Ideas for Incorporating Your Values into Your Life

Maybe none of these will grab you, but the hope is that they will open your mind and your heart to starting a new, healthier, more balanced, more tranquil, less stressed way of life.

1. Sign up for a class.
2. Laugh.
3. Make one choice to improve your health; ask a friend to be your "accountability buddy."
4. Spend time with a small child (consider borrowing one; the parents might appreciate the break).
5. Call a friend long-distance.
6. Ask for advice in starting a financial plan.
7. Watch a sunrise or sunset.
8. Make love.
9. Read a book for no practical purpose but enjoyment.
10. If quiet time is a value, figure out how you want to spend that quiet time (journaling? walking in nature?).
11. Ask someone you care about to introduce you to an activity that they love. This even works if that person is a little child.
12. Have lunch with a good friend or someone you'd like to know better.
13. Give a hug.
14. Receive a hug.
15. Make a list of your favorite activities (you might find clues from what you loved to do in your childhood).

16. Listen to your favorite music while doing nothing else for twenty minutes.
17. Do something you love to do.

During a dinner with friends, Eva shared that she remembers the delight of coloring books when she was little and it's reignited a whole new passion for her. A fellow asked her, "What are you doing? Taking painting or sketching classes?"

"No," said Eva, "I've finished four coloring books and have started a new one."

Maybe what you decide to add to your life might seem silly or childish to others, but why let that bother you? This is your self-care, your stress buster, your health, and your life. Forget what people might say or think, and take charge of starting to manage your stress.

But sometimes what we think is an important part of our lives turns out to be just a habit that does not reinvigorate us at all. Sam, a banker, was always tired, yet he claimed that he did take care of himself—his self-care plan was watching TV every night, because it relaxed him. Yet when his wife, Sheila, asked him a few questions, it turned out that there were very few shows that "sparked" him, that he was enthused about.

In fact, he felt that most of the shows were dumb or boring, but TV watching was his habit and he felt it would be a hard one to break. Sheila asked him if he realized that boredom is as exhausting as digging ditches. He said, "Now that you say that, I gotta admit, I agree." She asked what he loved to do as a kid or what he would love to do now.

He said, "The answer to both is build models. But when I get home from work I'm just too tired to do that." However, he asked his family to buy him a ship model for his birthday, and he surprised himself by starting to work on it a few days later.

"You're right," he told Sheila. "It gets my motor running again. I worked on the ship again last night and today I feel alive. And guess what. I still watched TV while I worked on it."

Light Up Your Life

Picture a continuum—a line with "burned out" at one end and "unlit" at the other. At the burned-out end, you have way too much to do, too many responsibilities, too many commitments.

The opposite of burnout is being uninspired. You wake up in the morning and there's no reason to get out of bed or to get dressed. There's no meaning in your life, no purpose. And you are bored.

In a seminar, a woman talked of being exhausted all the time. "Could you be bored?" I asked.

"No way," she barked, and then she whipped out from her purse her long list of things to do that day.

"Is there anything you enjoy on there?" I persisted. She told the whole group that no, there was nothing on that list that she liked to do. Day after day, she spent hours doing nothing but drudgery or hated chores. Well, that's boredom.

If you're at either extreme, the result is exhaustion. Bone-numbing, lean-against-the-wall-and-you'll-fall-asleep exhaustion. Either way, you are tired and don't care about much. Your mission is to find balance, the spot on that line where you're not uninspired, where there's enough going on in your life that it has meaning and purpose, but you're not so busy that you are sleep deprived or dragging around weary to the core of your being—burned out.

WHAT LIGHTS YOU UP?

Here are some sample answers:

cooperation	a handwritten letter
finding a hobby	teamwork
building a fire in a fireplace	seasonal changes
crossing out the last thing on a to-do list	music
	new challenges
warm sunny days	meaningful work
vacation	bubble baths
payday	shopping
pets	a bottle of wine
thank-yous	no traffic
variety	achieving personal goals
going out to lunch	Cubs win
clean bedsheets	reconciliation with a friend
shopping	cold beer on a hot day
success at work	hot chocolate on a cold day
success at home	

WHAT BURNS YOU OUT?

Here are some sample answers:

guilt trips	working in crisis
crabby people	bad luck
conflicting schedules	traffic
financial concerns	bad weather
a too-crowded schedule	lack of sleep or exercise
computer problems	too much e-mail/voice mail
toxic people	working when sick
lack of appreciation	no vacations
long hours	repetition (same ol' same ol')
negativity	not enough time for
balancing family and work	personal growth

That balance spot on the line between burned out and unlit will vary from day to day, and your center of balance will be different from other people's. What's right for one person might be wrong for you. In one of my seminars, Maya explained that her mother would look at her spot of balance and say, "Too much going on; too many activities. I would burn out." Yet her daughter is the opposite. She wants more activities, her mother wants less.

You have to find your own balance spot.

Hidden Benefits of Volunteering

Jill, a corporate executive, found herself obsessing about the plight of the homeless and the poor in Africa, then eventually the plight of the world. During a conversation with Hannah, a longtime friend, Jill shared that not a day goes by that she doesn't feel anxiety and depression over these concerns.

Hannah commented that despite the fact that Jill is working in a corporate world that can tend to be self-centered, money grubbing, and uncaring, Jill has always valued helping others. Hannah said, "Jill, anytime a person frets or worries about world problems, the solution is for them to do something, no matter how small, to make this a better world."

Jill countered that she didn't have time, and besides, through her business, she was making this a better world in many ways, such as aiding the economy and providing top-quality products.

Hannah said, "Yes, and you're getting paid very, very well for it. I'm suggesting you volunteer some time for a worthy cause and perhaps start regularly donating money to a charity that means something to you. Honest, Jill, you'll be amazed at how your anxiety will melt away once you start giving back."

Jill brushed aside her friend's suggestions because she absolutely had no spare time and really didn't agree with Hannah's theory, so she changed the subject.

The following week Henry, a co-worker, sent a group e-mail quoting a book called *Margin* by Richard A. Swenson, M.D.: "A University of Michigan study followed 2,700 people for over a decade to see how their social relationships affected their health and well-being. Those who performed regular volunteer work showed dramatically increased life expectancy. Men not involved in such altruistic activity had two-and-one-half times the morbidity during the period studied than those who volunteered at least once a week."

At the end of this e-mail, Henry invited everyone to join him that weekend building a house with Habitat for Humanity. Jill joined the group. By Sunday night, she was aching and exhausted but she felt that she had just made a great contribution to the world. And she understood Hannah's thinking. If you are upset with the world, do something to help it.

Within months, Jill had a new routine. She can't afford to give whole weekends to building houses, so she volunteers at a homeless shelter two evenings per month, gives time to Habitat for Humanity once in a while, and joined Women for Women, through which she donates a certain amount of money every month to support a woman in Nigeria. She exchanges letters and photos with her "foster sister" and is learning about positive programs being offered to women in third-world countries.

The odd thing is, even though she is learning more and more about difficulties among less-fortunate people, she no longer experiences anxiety and depression about the world. She feels terrific.

Jill was able to include her values into her lifestyle as a busy corporate executive. What happens if *you* can't? Sometimes circumstances simply will not allow us—for now—to do that. That's OK. It is still beneficial to explore, identify, and clarify your values.

Like a single mom who values painting landscapes but cannot carve out the time for it, or a husband and wife who cherish time together but spend every waking moment either at work or caring for elderly parents, what is important to you is sometimes temporarily unavailable. But as long as those values are clear in their minds, the mom might find a minute or two occasionally to sketch a beautiful scene and the couple might sneak in a few magic moments together.

William Butler Yeats wrote a poem when he was standing on the gray pavements of London; he reflected on how much he loved and valued the lake island of Innisfree in his homeland of Ireland. He missed the simplicity and peaceful, quiet life, and although he wasn't in a position to return to Innisfree, he went there in his mind.

The Lake Isle of Innisfree
BY WILLIAM BUTLER YEATS

I will arise and go now, and go to Innisfree,
And a small cabin build there, of clay and wattles made;
Nine bean rows will I have there, a hive for the honey bee,
And live alone in the bee-loud glade.

And I shall have some peace there, for peace comes dropping slow,
Dropping from the veils of the morning to where the cricket sings;
There midnight's all a glimmer, and noon a purple glow,
And evening full of the linnet's wings.

I will arise and go now, for always night and day
I hear lake water lapping with low sounds by the
    shore;
While I stand on the roadway, or on the pavements
    gray,
I hear it in the deep heart's core.

That's really what we are searching for in this chapter. What brings peace and serenity to your deep heart's core? Your children or grandchildren? Your pets? Music, art, learning? Something spiritual, intellectual, emotional, or physical?

We might not always be able to access what we love when we need it, but there's no reason why you can't just experience it in your mind as Yeats did. You might be surprised at how visualizing a peaceful setting can be as soothing as actually being there.

THOUGHTS TO PONDER

If you want to be successful, it's just this simple. Know
what you are doing. Love what you are doing. And
believe in what you are doing.

            —WILL ROGERS

There is only one success—to be able to spend your life
in your own way.

            —CHRISTOPHER MORLEY

Life isn't a matter of milestones but of moments.
—Rose Fitzgerald Kennedy

Things that matter most must never be at the mercy of things that matter least.
—Johann Wolfgang von Goethe

I firmly believe the Universe dreams a bigger dream for you than you can dream for yourself . . . You've got to open yourself to the dream that the Universe has for you. You've got to discover your true calling.
—Oprah Winfrey

The only ones among us who will be truly happy are those who have sought and found how to serve.
—Albert Schweitzer

To be happy at home is the ultimate result of all ambition.
—Samuel Johnson

Humankind has not woven the web of life.
We are but one thread within it.
Whatever we do to the web, we do to ourselves.
All things are bound together.
All things connect.
—Chief Seattle

Only you can be yourself. No one else is qualified for the job.

—ANONYMOUS

The bitterest tears shed over graves are for words left unsaid and deeds left undone.

—HARRIET BEECHER STOWE

You cannot live a perfect day without doing something for someone who will never be able to repay you.

—JOHN WOODEN

I have found that if you love life, life will love you back.

—ARTHUR RUBINSTEIN

The game of life is the game of boomerangs. Our thoughts, deeds, and words return to us sooner or later, with astounding accuracy.

—FLORENCE SCOVEL SHINN

One's philosophy is not best expressed in words; it is expressed in the choices one makes . . . The process never ends until we die. And the choices we make are ultimately our responsibility.

—ELEANOR ROOSEVELT

Love people and use things
Not the other way around.

—ANONYMOUS

EXTRA CREDIT

Questions About Values to Ponder

1. Is all your time being spent on unimportant stuff? Are you racing through life chasing things you don't value or care about?
2. List your top values:

_____

_____

_____

_____

3. How much time are you spending on that which is most important to you? How much time are you spending on that which is least important to you?
4. If you are not living according to your values, uncover what is keeping you from doing so. Is it time? Money? Energy? Are expectations holding you back? Whose expectations? (Family? Work? The world? Yours, maybe?)

_____

_____

_____

5. What can you do to start spending some time in an effective, positive, battery-charging manner?

_____

_____

_____

6. Are you putting off happiness? Relaxation? Rest?
7. Are you making yourself miserable by trying to make everybody happy?

CHAPTER 3

Trash Perfectionism

RAINA, A WEDDING PHOTOGRAPHER, WAS chatting with me after hearing one of my keynote presentations and casually mentioned, "My house is always a mess because I'm a perfectionist."

Doesn't that sound backward to you? Wouldn't you think that a perfectionist would have a house that is always immaculate?

But Raina went on to explain, "My mother taught me that the right way to wash the kitchen floor is to move the table and chairs aside, and the right way to vacuum is to move every piece of furniture. So if I don't have the time or energy to do it right, I don't do it at all."

Do you put off doing something until you have the time and energy to do it perfectly? Then you beat up on yourself and get stressed out because it's still not done? Do you expect yourself to be perfect . . . always?

Julia Cameron, in her book *The Artist's Way: A Spiritual Path to Higher Creativity*, says, "Perfectionism is not a quest for the best. It is a pursuit of the worst in ourselves, the part that tells us that nothing we do will ever be good enough."

When we were in school, we were given rules for becoming a perfect student. Later, there were criteria for being the perfect worker, spouse, partner, and parent. Eventually we become convinced that perfection is a desirable goal.

Well, here's the news flash. Striving for perfection in yourself will cause stress. Perfectionists focus on the flaws and feel agitated over what is not acceptable in their eyes. Not only is this not desirable, perfection is seldom attainable in yourself or others.

If you expect perfection in your family, friends, co-workers, or others, you will always be disappointed, frustrated, and stressed, because nobody is perfect. And as a by-product, you will make them crazy. When you expect people to be perfect, you cause them to feel inferior, inadequate, and sometimes angry. This not only damages their self-esteem and diminishes their performance, it perpetuates a cycle of frustration that further increases the stress level for all involved.

People will make mistakes, let you down, act goofy. You will try to teach someone how to do something "the right way" (your way) and they will do it "the wrong way" (their way). Life is too short to spend it being stressed and frustrated because others aren't perfect.

If you are often frustrated beyond belief by the incompetence of others around you or their meanness or lack of caring, you need to release, relax, and let go. Yes, there are many people less competent and less intelligent than you. Yes, there are many who are cruel or don't care as much or about the same things as you. But isn't it also true that there are many who are more competent and more intelligent than you, and who are kinder, more caring, and more giving than you? Accepting people's different levels of accomplishment and ways of doing things can go a long way in reducing your stress level.

Perfection Is Not the Measure of Success

Strive for excellence instead of perfection. Excellence is achievable; perfection seldom is. A manufacturer's rep once asserted in a seminar that the product she represented was a perfect achievement. Another member of the seminar asked her if the manufacturer had a research and development department. The answer was yes, and the fellow replied, "Well, then, that department is working to improve that product. Therefore, even they don't consider it to be perfect. Right?"

Pursuing excellence will allow you to continue to strive for success (however you may define it) without stressing over what is beyond your control.

Yeprem, an artist, saw a wooden plaque at a craft show and bought it. He meditates on this plaque's inscription at least once a week:

WHAT IS SUCCESS?

Setting Goals
But not in concrete
Staying Focused
But turning aside to help someone
Following a Plan
But remaining flexible

Moving Ahead
But not too fast to smell the flowers
Taking a Bow
But applauding those who had a part in your success

On her TV talk show, Oprah Winfrey was interviewing Colin Cowie, who she called a "master party planner." They were showing some of the spectacular weddings that he had put together, and Oprah asked Colin what he replies when a bride says, "I want the perfect wedding."

Without hesitation, Colin said, "You came to the wrong man. I don't do perfect. I can't do perfect but I will give you a piece of my heart, a piece of my soul, and an inch of my hairline. Your best in life is really good enough."

Are your expectations ridiculously high for activities or events you've planned? Roger, a plant manager, kept assuring his daughter as her wedding day drew near, "Everything's going to be perfect." He was generating an expectation that was a setup for disaster. On the day of the wedding, every little minor thing that went wrong turned into a major disappointment—not just for his daughter, but for his whole family, because they were expecting perfection.

On the other hand—in another family—when Gina threw a bridal shower for her kid sister, Angelina, she asked everyone to write out their favorite wedding "horror story" and she assembled them all into a notebook. The room rocked with laughter as they related stories of cakes falling, fights, police being called, rain, snow, missing wedding rings, flower girls' giggle fits, and ring bearers' "potty needs."

On the day of Angelina's wedding, when her flowers couldn't be found, she sighed and said, "I haven't even walked down the aisle yet, and already I have my story to tell." People in the family and wedding party were slightly upset, but not nearly as stressed as the family of Roger.

You may have memories of a perfect holiday or party or vacation, but if you could rerun that event, you probably would see that not every moment was ideal—and the event was still memorable and successful.

Don't Suffer in Perfect Silence

We sometimes become overwhelmed because we are too concerned about being thought of as the perfect employee or volunteer when something *less* self-sacrificing would be completely acceptable. Here's a charming tale about St. Patrick and a king named Angus that can illustrate this point.

At the Rock of Cashel in County Tipperary, Ireland, they say that Patrick was the bishop officiating at the coronation ceremony of Angus, around the year 440 A.D. People had traveled for days, coming from miles away, to sit on the grass and experience this important day for their new king, who they were so fond of.

The opening of the ceremony called for Bishop Patrick to lift his huge shepherd's staff and thump it into the ground three times.

Thump! Thump! Thump!

With the third thump, the bishop's staff accidentally pierced right through the foot and sandal of Angus. Bishop Patrick didn't notice it, and Angus never let out a sound, but he was suffering pain like he had never imagined. His foot was pinned to the ground, and every nerve in his body throbbed in agony.

At the close of the ceremony—*three and a half hours later*— poor Angus was supposed to kneel, kiss the bishop's ring, and then turn to greet his followers for the first time officially as their king. In excruciating torment and wracked with pain, Angus leaned forward and whispered, "I can't kneel; I can't turn around."

Shocked, the bishop asked, "Why not?"

Angus looked down at his foot, which was now swollen and had turned black, yellow, and blue. Horrified at seeing the pool of blood and the wounded, discolored foot of the king, Patrick asked, "Why didn't you tell me?"

Angus softly replied, "I thought it was part of the ceremony."

You may be silently enduring difficult working conditions, abusive relationships, or an excessive workload because you "thought it was part of the ceremony." In some instances, your supervisor (or the head of your committee) might not be aware of how overburdened you are. She might say, "I wish I knew what you were going through. Why didn't you say something?"

If you're suffering because you have too much to do at work, at home, or in volunteer activities, speak up. Don't suffer in silence, telling yourself, "I thought this was how it was supposed to be."

Keeping Up the Appearance of Busy-ness

How many hours per day do you put in at work? Are you exhausted and frazzled because you can never break away from the phone, e-mail, texting, and BlackBerry?

The problem is not your lack of time, it is how you use that time. What matters is not how much you work but what you accomplish. And sometimes our expectation of ourselves isn't to be productive, it is to look busy. This can be true even when nobody sees it but you.

Shift your focus to being more productive. Start by prioritizing your work. Be selective about the phone calls you'll accept when you are away from work and about how much work you'll do at home. Business guru Peter Drucker wrote, "Nothing is less productive than to make more efficient what should not be done at all."

Sometimes people knock themselves out working extra hours because they truly believe that their boss or the company expects it of them. But nobody expects you to work 24/7. You are simply living up to your own expectations—trying to be perfect.

Sue, a credit union supervisor, said in a stress management class that she took great pride in not having taken a lunch break in the eight years she had been in her position. When the group questioned her, she explained she felt the company probably expected that of her. After further questions, she finally admitted that the other supervisors did take lunch breaks and had given up inviting Sue to join them.

After a brief class discussion about stress and expectations, Sue made a resolution that before our next class meeting, she would tear herself away from her desk at lunchtime. The following week she reported back her "shocking news" that she went out to lunch and no one cared that she was away from her desk. Nobody commented or questioned her about it. She sheepishly admitted that she "sort of" had an image that her staff and the board of directors all admired her and appreciated her dedication. Sue said, "All these years of not taking breaks—no appreciation, no compensation. Nobody even noticed. And when I asked myself why I made that decision for eight years, I honestly didn't have an answer. I was just doing what I thought a perfect supervisor was supposed to do. But I don't know where I thought that 'rule' came from. I wonder if—deep down, subconsciously—I thought the place would fall apart without me if I left during lunchtime."

Do you relate? Have you ever gone to work despite being sick as a dog (and watched the smiles of appreciation as you shared your germs with everyone)? Or missed an important social or family event because work interfered?

Do you believe deep down that your place of business will fall apart if you stop doing what you are doing? Or that maybe your family will fall apart, or your religious or civic association cannot manage unless you plan and work tirelessly for it?

Unrealistic expectations can keep you awake at night thinking about what you didn't do today and still have to do tomorrow. They can push you to exhaustion. Expectations of yourself can cause so much stress that you get sick or depressed.

WHAT HAS CONTROL OVER YOUR LIFE THAT MIGHT CAUSE YOU STRESS?

priorities of others

demands of others

e-mails

a manipulative relative

job

boss

limiting beliefs

fears

procrastination

addictions

The Control Freak and the Fervent Fixer

One of the biggest causes of stress and burnout is trying to control an inflexible environment or the people in it. When you try to control something or someone that you really don't have *any* control over, the result is always stress for you and sometimes stress for others. It's called being a Control Freak. When you finally realize, understand, and admit to yourself that you have no control over that person, place, or thing, you let go. You let go of control. You let go of the pain of unrealistic expectations of perfection. You let go of stress.

A variation on the Control Freak is the Fervent Fixer, the person who sees a problem and is determined to fix it—whether people want it fixed or not. It is common for a woman who is describing a problem at work to her boyfriend or husband to become frustrated if her mate keeps trying to offer solutions. The woman wants to discuss the process of what is going on, but the man is a Fervent Fixer and wants to solve the problem. Often an argument (or stress) results.

Of course, when Fervent Fixers see a problem they can solve, life is good. But if they expect perfection of themselves and want to fix everything, it's inevitable that sometimes they'll come upon an unfixable problem.

The Fizzle Factor

Michael, a twenty-seven-year old financial adviser, was helping to set up for an all-day seminar he was going to co-lead with his father. Suddenly his dad realized he was missing some material that accounted for two hours of the seven-hour program. He started a frantic search and Michael, looking concerned, walked over and asked if he could help.

His dad said no and Michael calmly walked away. I asked him if any of us could offer to help and Michael said, "No, wait till he fizzles."

Everyone in the room stopped what they were doing and all eyes were on Michael.

"Fizzles?" a woman asked.

He said, "Yeah, you know. Don't you have times where you are so frantic looking for something that if someone gets in your way, you practically knock them over? Or if they say something to you and interrupt your thoughts, you practically bite their head off? Well, at those times, I just keep out of the way and wait till they fizzle. Heck, I don't want to be knocked over or have my head chewed off."

One of the men commented, "You know, I think that's what we need to do when our kids throw a tantrum or get all wound up over something. I always try to be the perfect dad and step in to fix things—you know, calm them down. And usually I just make matters worse, but could never think of what else to do.

"I should just get out of the way till they fizzle."

Instead of rushing in and trying to make everything perfect by fixing things with someone who is frantic or upset, simply offer help, let them know you are available if they need your help or support, and then get out of the way until they're ready to accept your assistance.

Don't Fall for the Myth of "Fairy-Tale People"

Did you ever think someone had a perfect relationship, job, partner, home, situation, life? Or have you ever thought, "If I had what that person has, my life would be perfect and I would never have any problems, worries, or sadness"? Then, when you got to know her better, you discovered that she has the same aches and pains, ups and downs, joys and frustrations, griefs, struggles, and trials as you and everyone else?

Fairy tales program our minds to believe that if certain things happen, then people get to live happily ever after. But no matter what we do or how hard we work, we never achieve the perfection that we believe others have.

People who are obsessed with how they are perceived want the world to think their life circumstances are perfect and they work hard to create that illusion. They are likely to respond to situations that could tarnish their image by saying things like, "I hope your grandmother never finds out you have a tattoo" or "How could you call me that in front of people?" (as if it's just fine to call them that when you're alone) or "Don't ever tell anyone this happened, OK?" or "You told your teacher *what*!!?"

Barb, an options broker, described how she and two friends were discussing some holiday letters she had received from people who listed all the activities their children were involved with. During the conversation, one of her friends blurted out, "They're Fairy-Tale People! They're people who are always trying to convince you—in holiday letters or not—that they have perfect children, a perfect marriage or family, or are perfect parents. They're trying to convince you that they are living happily ever after— like they're in a fairy tale!"

Barb added, "Maybe we're all that way. On one vacation we had several arguments, fights, disagreements, whatever you want to call them. But when people asked how was our vacation, I always said it was great. Why couldn't I just be honest?"

The three women decided together that in addition to those who *claim* to be perfect, those who *strive* to be perfect or to have a perfect life also are Fairy-Tale People. They are trying to live happily ever after in an imperfect world—they're headed for disappointment and heartache. After that discussion, Barb made some major changes. She started by changing her expectations of herself and her family.

Are you starting to see the power that perfectionism has over us? How much of an impact your expectations of perfection have on creating stress in your life? And the fairy tales don't stop with you or those around you. You might find yourself becoming stressed when you convince yourself that this house or apartment is going to be perfect, or this job, boss, location, situation—anything.

It's fairy-tale thinking that creates the "honeymoon's over" type of stress. You know that feeling when you start to see the flaw in something for the first time? When that new wonderful co-worker or friend betrays you. When those sensational new shoes become furiously uncomfortable after twenty minutes of wearing them. When your perfect new software acts like a cranky kid with a mind of its own and simply refuses to do something you really really want it to do. When your dream vacation is rained out day after day. When you stumble across a flaw in anything, you need to remind yourself that there is an upside and a downside to every single thing and situation in life. And most things are not perfect.

NINETEEN WAYS TO STRESS OUT A PERFECTIONIST TO THE POINT OF MADNESS

1. Put empty cartons and bottles back into the fridge.
2. If someone is telling a joke and you've heard it before, wait until they're nearly finished and then shout out the punch line.
3. Take every opportunity to give the perfectionist advice. Especially on subjects you know nothing about.
4. Squeeze the toothpaste tube from the middle. Never replace the cap.
5. Always be late.
6. Go to the movies with your perfectionist and just keep chatting.

7. When people gather at your perfectionist's place, constantly bring the conversation around to sex, politics, or religion. Preferably all three.

8. If your perfectionist is single, frequently ask with a big smile, "So when are you getting married?" And, of course, if they are newly married, you've got to ask, "So when is the baby coming?"

9. If your perfectionist does have a child, give a sweet little puppy as a birthday gift . . . or a kitten.

10. Borrow money often from your perfectionist and forget to pay it back.

11. Recognize your limitations. Then ignore them.

12. Recognize your perfectionist's limitations. Then tell him or her what they are.

13. Never return anything you borrow.

14. Give your perfectionist a double espresso just before bedtime.

15. Switch around the decaffeinated and caffeinated coffee every chance you get.

16. Turn on and turn up all the appliances in any room you are in. Leave them on.

17. Keep a photo of your past lover where your current lover is bound to see it.

18. Constantly raise the hopes of your perfectionist that you are going to mend your ways and improve. Then take every opportunity to dash those hopes.

19. Always make sure you have the last word.

Where Do Your Expectations Come From?

There isn't one clear source for where your expectations of perfection come from. These "rules" that are rattling around in your brain could come from your childhood, a comment you overheard at work, your best friend's pet peeve, or even television.

Pay attention to how holidays are portrayed on TV. Everyone is so very, very happy, the decorations are . . . well . . . perfect, and the time spent together is so very, very enjoyable. We are smart enough to know that is unrealistic, but on the other hand, isn't that a principle of brainwashing? Keep repeating something over and over until people start to believe it, and often the result is we expect family, meals, decorations, weather—even the poor turkey—to be perfect.

So when your holiday is less than perfect—Auntie had a bit too much to drink, your uncle is arguing with everyone, the kids are running through the house screaming at the top of their lungs with your pitted olives poked on their fingertips, something navy blue is all over the carpet, the marshmallows on the sweet potatoes are golden black—do you find yourself wondering "Where did I go wrong?"

Real life seldom reflects what we've been watching on TV or those fantasy memories of celebrations from our childhood.

Thoughts to Ponder

Perfectionism is the voice of the oppressor, the enemy of the people. It will keep you cramped and insane your whole life.

—Anne Lamott

If everything's under control, you're going too slow.

—Mario Andretti

I will tell you that there have been no failures in my life. I don't want to sound like some metaphysical queen, but there have been no failures. There have been some tremendous lessons.

—Oprah Winfrey

I wish someone would tell us from the beginning that we are dying. Then we wouldn't be afraid to really live.

—Michael Landon

Life's journey is not to arrive at the grave safely in a well-preserved body, but rather to skid in sideways, totally worn out, shouting, "Woo hoo . . . what a ride!"

—Anonymous

Unless you're willing to have a go, fail miserably, and have another go, success won't happen.

—Phillip Adams

The thing that is really hard, and really amazing, is giving up on being perfect and beginning the work of becoming yourself.

—ANNA QUINDLEN

Being happy doesn't mean everything's perfect. It means you've decided to see beyond the imperfections!

—HELEN KELLER

EXTRA CREDIT

1. Who's in control in your life?

_____

_____

_____

2. What are you trying to control that's uncontrollable?

_____

_____

_____

3. What is within your control?

_____

_____

_____

4. What controls you (phone, schedule, computer, demands of others, e-mails)?

_____

_____

_____

5. What impossible standards do you strive for (perfection, never making a mistake)?

_____

6. Think of a few times you've been very upset over a person or event. List them.

_____

_____

_____

_____

_____

7. Were you upset because you expected perfection?

CHAPTER 4

Reach for Realistic Goals That Are Both Relevant and Rewarding

WHEN THE DOCTOR TOLD EILEEN that her mother's Alzheimer's disease had progressed to the point where she had to be put in a nursing home, Eileen had a clear goal in mind. She was going to take a leave of absence and give her mother the very best care possible, and prove to the professionals that her mother did not need to go into a nursing home. After all, if her mother could manage to raise and care for five kids, certainly one of those kids would be able to care for her. Eileen even wrote out her plan for giving care to her mom. It was a carefully thought-out goal—one that she could carry out on her own, without help from anyone.

The problem was, it was an unrealistic goal. Five weeks later, Eileen's blood pressure was soaring, she was battling acid reflux, and then she landed in bed with a serious case of the flu. The doctor said the reason it was taking her so long to recover was that stress and fatigue had weakened her immune system. And he suspected that her anger with her four siblings also contributed to her illness. Eileen was furious with them because all they ever did was squeeze in a few quick visits per week.

Eileen shared with the doctor her goal of being the sole, superior caregiver for her mom and explained it wasn't her nature to ask for help. But the doctor pointed out that if Eileen didn't start to take care of her stress, she might get seriously ill and not be at all available to her mother. He strongly urged her to talk to her siblings and ask them to join in with giving care to their mother.

After much internal struggle, Eileen set new—more realistic—goals, including talking to her brothers and sisters about how difficult life had been with their mother and how she was seeking help. All four were shocked. They each described how they thought Eileen was so totally self-sufficient that they didn't think she needed anything. Her big brother said, "Eileen, how are we supposed to know that you need help if you don't tell us? I'm there for you but you have to spell out what *kind* of help you need. Then I'm glad to be part of taking care of Mom."

They all wanted to help, and once each of them figured out what they could do—everything from cleaning Eileen's house and yard to staying with Mom so Eileen could have some time off or running errands for her—Eileen's life became simpler. They enrolled their mom in an adult day-care center, but over time, as their mother deteriorated, the five of them agreed—although sadly and reluctantly—that she would best be cared for by professionals in a long-term care facility.

Now Eileen and her siblings visit every day and make certain that their mom is well cared for. They are at peace with their decision and their mother seems to be at peace in her new home.

Often the goal that seems so kind and noble turns out to be unrealistic. Note that Eileen's goal of giving the best of care wasn't the unrealistic part at that stage of her mom's illness; it was trying to do it all on her own that did her in.

Sometimes it is your goal that causes stress; sometimes it is merely the way you plan to achieve your goal that frustrates you.

TIPS FOR CAREGIVERS

1. Take care of yourself; get enough rest and sleep. This is not a luxury, it's a necessity.
2. Find someone to talk to, perhaps a support group or an understanding friend.
3. Be social; don't become a recluse. Keep up with your friends.
4. Learn to ask for help: www.eldercare.gov is a place to start searching for local agencies such as Meals on Wheels, home health aides, and adult day care facilities. Keep asking different people till you get the help you need.
5. Stay emotionally healthy—change the scene, go for a walk, get fresh air. Don't feel guilty for taking time for yourself. Staying emotionally healthy will make you a better caregiver.
6. Stay physically healthy—eat a balanced diet and get some exercise. Consider learning yoga for mental, physical, and spiritual health.
7. Keep laughter and music in your life. When tensions run high and energy runs low, listening to uplifting music, watching a comedy, or simply seeing the absurdity of life can keep you sane.

8. Find a way to express yourself: Journaling can be a great release for frustration.

9. Have a life outside the caretaker role: Take time off to keep up with hobbies and interests or do something you enjoy.

10. Appreciate the good moments.

11. Search for helpful resources such as the Alzheimer's Association's Helpline (800-272-3900).

12. Treat yourself to something occasionally. You deserve it.

Positive and Negative Goals

Did you ever set a goal and wonder why nothing ever came of it? For example, sometimes people make New Year's resolutions to become happier or lose weight or increase their self-confidence. Or perhaps you have more specific goals, such as starting a new business, having weekly meetings with a colleague, or getting your mother-in-law to like you, but still nothing happens. Many people think that any goal they set is better than nothing, that all goals are positive. Not true.

A goal can be negative or unrealistic if . . .

• the action is out of your control. You have control over reaching out to your mother-in-law or being friendlier, but you cannot control whether she likes you. Some people will never like you no matter *how* kind you are to them. You may want to have a meeting with someone, but if she has the control over saying yes or no, you control only the option of inviting her. So more positive goals would be for you to invite your colleague to a meeting and to act in a different way with your mother-in-law.

· the action is not specific or there's no time limit. If you say, "I will start a new business," that's too vague. You must outline the steps you need to take and put them in sequence. Break the action down into incremental stages and then follow your plan. For example, your first positive, specific goal might be: By March 17, I will sign up for an evening accounting class and will have called a real estate agent to help me find the right location. If your goal is to lose weight, specify how many pounds by a certain date. Otherwise, the criteria for success are too vague. Losing one pound in a month is not much of a goal, but aiming for twenty pounds in two weeks is totally unrealistic.

· the outcome is not measurable. If becoming more confident is your goal, how will you know when you've achieved it? If you confidently say no to a telemarketer? For "becoming more confident" to be a measurable, positive goal, you have to define what behavior would be an example of your having gained confidence. Do you want to call someone and ask him to attend a party with you? Do you want to be able to give a presentation to your co-workers? Do you want to go for a job interview without having major anxiety attacks or collapsing in a heap outside the interviewer's door? Add a date to that behavior and you have a positive, measurable goal. "I will say yes to giving a talk at our annual meeting in June," or "By January 15, I will volunteer to serve on the board of my association."

Once you learn to reach for specific and measurable goals that are within your control, you will no longer be setting negative goals. You'll be reaching for positive goals that are realistic, relevant, and rewarding.

People tend to assign goals to most activities, but they do it unconsciously without realizing that they are actually goal setting. Reggie talked of attending a chamber of commerce meeting with the hope (goal) of meeting fellow leaders in his new community. Many at his table had the same desire (goal). But the meeting planner's agenda (goal) was to pack as much information into as many speeches as possible. As a result there was no time for networking, so the attendees tried to carry on conversations during the program, which was extremely distracting to the speakers.

In the end, everyone was stressed—the attendees, who didn't get a chance to meet each other; the speakers, who felt they didn't give their best presentation due to the distracting conversations; and the meeting planner, who set a goal that contradicted the goals of the members.

Recognizing that we have goals—conscious or subconscious—for everything we do can help us eliminate many of our negative goals.

Goal Stoppers

Emmett's Law of Goal Setting: As soon as you set a goal that is important to you, equally important obstacles start popping up all over the place.

Has something like this ever happened to you: You decide with all your heart that you are going to lose weight and then a loving friend gives you a box of your favorite candy or some homemade fudge? Or you're struggling to quit smoking and your pal brings you three cartons of your brand because he was in another state where they sold cigarettes dirt cheap? I hear stories like this all the time. Sometimes we wonder if others are trying to sabotage our goals, but usually it's just that a person didn't have a clue that we were determined to finally make that change.

I call these crazy incidents "goal stoppers." They are not the same as phony excuses and they are not caused by us. They come from outside our control.

There are many explanations and theories about why this happens, but the important thing is to recognize when you are in a goal-stopper situation and figure out how to get around it.

Goal stoppers almost torpedoed me when I thought maybe I'd start writing my first book, *The Procrastinator's Handbook*. First came some family illnesses, and then I was in a serious auto accident, followed by even more painful occurrences. In a three-month period, my mother passed away, my father-in-law passed away, and my twenty-five-year marriage ended.

Writing became the last thing on my mind. Maybe I could have found time to write during this period, but I didn't have the emotional energy to think straight and focus on anything.

Years later, once I regained my balance and again decided to start my masterpiece, my daughter got married and I met a man in the cat food aisle at the grocery store and fell in love (with him, not the cat food). Again—enormous emotions. Even though the emotions were happy, they were goal stoppers. Still no book.

All of these goal stoppers were real and extremely important to me, not mealy-mouthed excuses. But still—no book. Finally, in 1994, Bruce (the cat-food-aisle guy) and I married. Life was good. More emotions, but what about the book?

With great determination, I decided to find the time to start writing. That year and the next, two of our sons got married. I finally figured out that life will *always* have important and powerful ups and downs. So to defeat goal stoppers, I decided to carve out one hour per week to write.

Great plan, yes? The very first hour of my very first week, the phone rang. I decided to ignore it. And on the answering machine I heard a dear friend sobbing. She had never before in the life of our friendship called in tears. I answered it. As we talked, I tucked away my notes about the book . . . and forgot about them.

A year later I still had not begun writing my book. Later that week, when I was floating on a caffeine high and could not fall asleep, I decided to get up in the middle of the night and put in an hour on my book. And that was the breakthrough. I put in an hour a week for the next four weeks; then I was on my way and the goal stoppers stopped stopping my book.

When sabotaging goal stoppers assault you, the first thing to do is recognize what is happening and know that it happens to all of us many times in our lives. The next thing to do is figure out a way to take one small step toward your goal. See if you can find a way to sidestep the goal stoppers (like my writing in the middle of the night). It seems that once you take that one small step, you loosen the hold goal stoppers have on you.

At the end of this chapter, you will be asked to write down a goal you would like to achieve. Writing down goals is an important habit to form because having the goal in writing helps to remind you of it, so it doesn't fly out of your mind as soon as something else interesting flies in. Also, it helps keep you focused and moving forward with that goal. Many people report a sort of magic happens when they write goals. It's as if events and people seem to appear to help with that goal.

Consider starting a goal notebook. But your written goals don't have to be anything formal or fancy. Writing a goal on a Post-it note and smacking it on your bathroom mirror works wonderfully.

Life Goals Can Counterbalance Job Stress

Often people feel that they have no control over the direction their personal lives will take because they are too busy at work to have enough time and energy to set and strive toward nonwork goals. It never occurs to them that they can reach for life goals that would contribute to reducing their stress.

To presume that your personal life will go where you want it to go simply by default doesn't make sense. There are times when work goals that increase productivity will start making you crazy, stressed, or even sick. Those are times that you need to focus on nonwork life goals to keep yourself in balance and prevent burnout.

Pam, an administrative assistant, was having health problems from the stress of her job. She decided to reach for a goal to add joy and energy in her life. She knew she was never going to find ways to make her job enjoyable or less stressful, and yet she couldn't afford to quit, so she determined to streamline her after-work activities and trade two nights a week of TV for a stress-busting activity.

She made a list of what she valued in life and decided to join a volleyball team as a temporary activity till she found something to be enthusiastic about. She had loved playing volleyball in high school and felt she needed something physical to get her moving. She also made a commitment to volunteer one night a week at a local homeless shelter. Three years later, she is still with the shelter and still with the volleyball team, and feeling enthusiastic about both. The funny thing is, the team was started by a group of women who realized that just because their jobs were boring or stressful, their whole lives didn't have to be.

Pam says she has never been more energetic, healthy, or at ease with herself and life. Also she has lost twenty-seven pounds. If work stresses you, setting goals for your nonwork life can combat that stress and melt it away.

If you do not reach for goals to direct where your life is going, where will you end up? If you do not have specific goals, you will not have specific results. As you start the habit of reaching for realistic goals, remember that they can apply to all levels of your life. There is no reason why you cannot be reaching for goals for your career and finances, as well as goals for activities, people, and events in your life. You might even pursue a spiritual goal. For example, I often ask people in seminars how they want to be ten years from now and 92 percent have said they want to be more peaceful and serene, yet few people ever set a life goal of including more peace and serenity.

SIMPLE, RELEVANT, AND REWARDING LIFE GOALS

Learn to speak another language

Have a rose garden

Become a youth leader

Meet your favorite athlete

Stay at a luxurious hotel or spa

Donate regularly to your favorite charity

Join a spiritual group

Learn to dance

Buy your grandmother a flat-screen TV

Take a scenic train trip or a cruise

Go kayaking or snorkeling

Get financial advice from a successful millionaire

Learn to paint or take up another art form

Become a volunteer

Treat your mother to a day at a spa

Read the Bible or another holy text

Join a health club

Start a business

Buy books for orphaned children

Volunteer with Habitat for Humanity

Attend a ballet

Life Goals and the Good Old-Fashioned Work Ethic

People sometimes ask, "Why do I need to reach for goals in my life to prevent stress? Our grandparents worked hard and they never had to worry about stress, right? We'd all be better off if we had an old-fashioned work ethic like our grandparents. Maybe that's what the expression 'working 24/7' is bringing us back to."

Not true. Historically speaking, an old-fashioned work ethic meant work hard at work. It didn't mean work hard every hour of every day and schedule every minute of your life to be productive.

Many people can remember their grandparents or parents going out on the front porch after dinner and having neighbors and friends wander over to chat. If there was a sorrow in the family, this little community on the porch would grieve with you, and if there was a joy, they would celebrate with you.

John, a loan appraiser, talked about his grandparents playing cards with friends every Saturday night. He reassured us that his grandparents were very hard workers, but they didn't work seven days a week, and they always had time for family and friends. In spite of their goals of working hard and accomplishing a lot, they knew how to recharge their batteries on a regular basis.

Life in days of yore was lived to a different rhythm. Here's a great example of that difference. During the mid-1800s, a grandmother wrote out a list for her soon-to-be-married granddaughter, instructing her in seventeen steps how to do the laundry. This list was found in someone's attic trunk several years ago and has been reprinted in many magazines. It's a wonderful example of life's wisdom being passed from one generation to the next.

Step number one described how to build a fire in the backyard and make your own soap out of lye in a large cauldron. But the last two steps are what captured my imagination. Step number sixteen told the granddaughter to put the teakettle on the stove and to drag the rocking chair onto the front porch. Step number seventeen said, "Sip your tea, rock a little, relax and count your blessings."

What a different rhythm, a different attitude this displays than our generation's feelings toward work. Grandma was saying, "Oh, yes. Work hard. But when you're finished, part of the job is to relax."

That's certainly not how we approach work, is it? Our rhythm seems to be that we'll work, finish a project, hit the ground running, and jump right into another project. No time ever to "sip your tea, rock a little, relax and count your blessings."

Generations past have set the example of a good work ethic. After the hard work of a harvest came a feast or some kind of celebration. After a hard week's work, everyone gathered in town for a barn dance. After a hard day's work, the family would relax or play games or tell stories in the kitchen or around the fireplace. We never read about the mother jumping up and asking everyone to "hold that thought" while she runs down to the river to do another load of laundry.

A friend of mine has a sign on her desk that says:

When I work, I work hard
When I play, I play hard
And when I think, I sleep

Well, I'm not advocating that last line, but doesn't it make sense to keep work from taking over our leisure time? After doing hard work we need to relax, to "re-create" ourselves before we be-gin the next project in order to head off being steamrolled by stress.

The old-fashioned work ethic encouraged hard work, but it also nurtured the values of allowing people to rest, relax, and enjoy the company of others, and finding the solitude to read, pray, or think.

When Allen, a truck driver, told his teenage daughter Natalie that when he was a youngster, stores were closed on Sundays, she almost keeled over. In a shocked voice she said, "Yeah, but not the malls. The malls weren't closed, were they?" When he told her there *were* no malls when he was a kid, she was astounded. She told her dad she didn't know he was that old. (Allen decided to take that as a compliment.)

When Natalie asked what people did on Sundays, he told her that as a kid, he thought Sundays were very boring—the family went to church, read the paper, and relaxed, visited with friends, or had a big family dinner at Grandma's house.

"Oh, all the things people would love to do these days, but they don't have time," Natalie observed.

Yet no matter how boring Allen and other children may have thought Sundays were, people connected with friends, neighbors, or family, and they did something different from the rest of the week. Most important, they slowed down. How often have you ar-rived at work on Monday morning feeling exhausted from having been so busy all weekend?

Julie, a massage therapist, has a goal to keep Sundays free for family time. Her friends all know of Julie's goal, and when they ask to set a date to get together, they work around it.

If this seems too extreme for you, try setting a goal to mark occasional days on your calendar that are set aside just to relax. You will find that these help you to become more productive in the long run.

When Goals Match Your Values

If you get into the habit of including meaningful goals that are congruent with your values in all areas of your life, you will find yourself sidestepping tons of stress. For example, the family at Disney World with cranky kids whining and throwing tantrums and yelling parents who look frazzled and furious needs to evaluate its goals. Is the goal to get your money's worth and ride every single ride from early morning till they close at night? Or is the goal to have a good time with your children, which could mean taking a midday break and heading back to the motel for a refreshing dip in the pool or a nap, then perhaps returning in the late afternoon when it's a bit cooler and everyone has the energy to stay and enjoy the fireworks? Evaluating your goals can help make the difference between an enjoyable time with your family and a nightmare.

Hannah, who read in John Bradshaw's *Homecoming: Reclaiming and Healing Your Inner Child* the advice to "surround yourself with nourishing people, not toxic ones," thought about the people in her life. Every single one was a negative, complaining, *toxic* person. No wonder she was stressed out. She wasn't sure what to do, but she knew she had to make a plan (goal). She started with calling Mary Ann, an acquaintance she liked and admired. Hannah explained her situation and asked if they could get together occasionally to either play tennis or go to the movies.

Mary Ann wasn't into tennis but said she would love a pal to go to the movies with, so they set a date. Hannah said she felt as if she was in first grade asking someone if she would be her friend, but she was able to summon up the courage to make that call because she passionately wanted to change her life.

A friendship did develop between Hannah and Mary Ann, and both of them often talked about how to distance yourself from toxic people and associate with nourishing people. They knew they were stuck with their families but both belonged to negative, gossipy groups that they decided to drop. Also, they allowed some connections with several individuals to dwindle, and they started a women's group of other like-minded souls who supported and encouraged one another in reaching for their goal of redefining relationships in their lives to battle stress.

Setting Goals for Relationships Can Change Your Whole Life

Seven years ago, Jason and Tiffany were planning their wedding, and as the financial estimates mounted, Tiffany broke into tears from the stress of it all. "How can we afford all this?" she sobbed. "We'll be so far in debt, it will take us a lifetime to save the down payment for a house. I'm so stressed out spending all this money. I feel like a nervous wreck."

So Jason and Tiffany started a series of long discussions. Since the wedding is usually something the bride has been dreaming of,

Tiffany had to decide whether a huge wedding was more important to her than buying a house. She and Jason together had to
clarify what the purpose of their wedding was. Was it to impress
people and to spend a fortune or to provide a fun party to celebrate their commitment to each other? Tiffany recognized that
their purpose was to have a day of family, friends, and celebration
that they'd always remember, and impressing people and going
into debt weren't part of her vision.

As a result of goal setting, they decided to cut back on their
wedding not only to save money but also to make the wedding
planning more manageable for Tiffany, who was working full-
time and in the middle of taking her nursing board exams. Instead of spending for an extravagant cake, meals, and decor, they
chose simpler ways to go, but in the meantime searched the Inter-
net and asked friends and family about rituals and ceremonies to
include in their wedding day.

To this day, everyone remembers the "richness of joy and
memories" experienced at Jason and Tiffany's wedding: the special remembrances for the family members who had passed
away; Tiffany wearing her mother's headpiece and the gown
made by her two aunts; the special gifts presented to each set of
parents; and the "flock of flower girls"—all the nieces, each in her
own choice of pastel dress, fluttering up the aisle. Instead of expensive mementos for everyone, each guest received a candle,
and when the bride and groom danced for the first time as husband and wife, the lights dimmed and everyone lit their candle
and sent blessings upon the couple. Thanks to what they call
"Tiffany's Magic Meltdown" and the goal setting that resulted,
they planned a wedding they loved, didn't overspend, had a great

time themselves, and within a year and a half they had their down payment for a house.

Identifying your goals can help you in making big and little decisions. Hamid and his wife struggled with his decision to attend a conference. The cost of the conference was high, and when added to the cost of airfare, hotel, and meals, it was way more than they could afford, but he felt he would learn so much that he would earn back the conference cost within a month of returning home.

So Hamid attended the conference, met some terrific people, and attended some great presentations. When he came home, there was no change in his business practices or the success of his business. When his wife asked him what he specifically learned that would change the direction of his business, Hamid was stumped. If he had set realistic goals that were relevant (such as "improve marketing" or "learn to use technology to generate cash flow") he could have selected specific breakout sessions to gain the much-needed information and perhaps asked some of the new people he met to share their favorite marketing or technology tips.

Thinking about and setting goals can keep you from wasting money.

At a parents club meeting, Amber was talking with Trish about books, and Trish mentioned that her mother-in-law was a fairly successful published author. Amber said she'd love to meet her to ask her some questions about how to get published, but she didn't want to take advantage of her.

Trish said that since their boys were on the same baseball team, she and Amber could sit together during the next game. Even though her mother-in-law is a lawyer with a super-busy schedule, she would be there, too, so Amber could meet her and maybe make an appointment to ask questions about getting published.

At the game, when introduced to Trish's mother-in-law, Mrs. Clancy, Amber was astonished to recognize her. She sputtered, "Mrs. Clancy, haven't I seen you at every game this season? You practice law; you write books; how do you find the time to attend these games every week?"

Mrs. Clancy told her, "Well, I know what my values are and one of the top ones is family. So one of my goals is to make sure I spend time with them. This is a great way to do it. I get to cheer on Noah and his team, I get to sit and chat with the rest of the family, and afterward we all go out for pizza. Plus I get fresh air and sunshine. What could be a better use of my Saturday?"

Trish later said of her mother-in-law, "I'm astonished how much she accomplishes, but I know she writes out her goals and has a clear vision of what she wants in life. And many times I've seen her say no to something that would take her focus off what's important to her."

Footprints in the Snow

Once you clarify your values and then set goals to move toward the life you want, you need to write down your goals to help you keep your eyes on them. Mrs. Clancy often tells a story of three little kids who made a bet to see who could walk the straightest line from where they stood to a tree across a field of freshly fallen snow.

The first one kept her eyes on her feet as she put one foot cautiously in front of another. But when she got to the opposite end of the field, she looked up to see that instead of a straight line to the tree, she had walked at a slant that angled way off to the side.

Next a little boy started across the field. Learning from the girl's mistake, he kept looking back at his footprints in the snow and correcting his direction. When he got to the tree, his footprints formed a zigzag line all the way across.

The third one stepped onto the snow, fixed her eyes on the tree, and confidently and quickly walked across the field. When they looked at her footprints, she had walked a perfectly straight line.

When you have a clear vision of your goal, and you keep your eyes on it—instead of looking back at past mistakes or watching each step you take for fear of making a mistake—you will have a simpler, clearer path to accomplishing what you want in life.

Mrs. Clancy told the story to Trish's children many times, and the whole family was conscious of the value *and* the rewards of goal setting. By the way, Noah's team won the championship that year and Noah was voted most valuable player. Did it have anything to do with goals or footprints in the snow? Hmmm, you never know.

Remember to be vigilant in reevaluating your goals. If they are stress producing, they may be unrealistic goals. Sometimes a simple revision or adaptation of your goals can make the difference between stress and serenity.

THOUGHTS TO PONDER

Surround yourself with only people who are going to lift you higher.

—OPRAH WINFREY

Do nothing, and nothing happens. Do something, and something happens.

—BENJAMIN FRANKLIN

The question isn't who is going to let me; it's who is going to stop me.

—AYN RAND

*Wishing you a year that brings
True enjoyment in each moment,
True fulfillment in each goal,
True contentment in your heart,
And true delight within your soul*

—ANONYMOUS

The desire accomplished is sweet to the soul.

—KING SOLOMON

If you don't know where you are going, every road will get you nowhere.

—HENRY KISSINGER

Obstacles don't have to stop you. If you run into a wall, don't turn around and give up. Figure out how to climb it, go through it, or work around it.

—MICHAEL JORDAN

Make the most of yourself, for that is all there is of you.

—RALPH WALDO EMERSON

When you reach for the stars you may not quite get one, but you won't come up with a handful of mud either.

—LEO BURNETT

Obstacles are those frightful things you see when you take your eyes off your goals.

—HENRY FORD

EXTRA CREDIT

1. Have you ever reached for a goal that never came true? What was it?

_____

_____

_____

2. Do you have any idea why that goal never came to be? Was it unrealistic? Not within your control? Not specific or measurable?

Write your reason:

_____

_____

_____

3. What life goal or work goal would you like to achieve?

_____

_____

_____

4. Have you ever felt stressed due to a goal you pursued?

Do you recognize how—whether you realize it or not—all of us reach for goals in every area of our lives, even when attending a meeting or going to an amusement park? Have you uncovered any negative goals, such as working 24/7, trying for perfection, or allowing phones or computers to control every second of your life?

CHAPTER 5

Eliminate What You Can and Streamline Everything Else

WHILE ON A CRUISE TO ALASKA, Danny and Margaret went on a tour where they spotted a general store with a sign:

We have everything you need.
If we don't have it,
You don't need it.

When they told their fellow cruisers at dinner about the sign, everyone laughed. But then a discussion erupted about what people actually do need. Not just want, but need. All eight people at their table expressed an opinion.

Scott, a commodities broker, had been on a "wilderness experience" early in his career. He spent three days in the desert with only a knife and a blanket. He said it is astonishing to learn what we can do without—and although he wouldn't want to live that way, he thinks the experience colors his life decisions. For example, he just doesn't relate to the competitiveness and one-upmanship at work, and he doesn't care that his car is not top-of-the-line like those of his colleagues. But he maintained that everyone has their weird wants that have become needs to them, and for Scott it was high-tech toys.

Debbie asked what's wrong with having things that we might not need, but we want. She loves clothes, shoes, and jewelry and loves accumulating as much as she can. When her husband made a negative remark about Debbie's shoe collection, she countered with, "Please explain why we have four cars and only two drivers in the family."

To head off their bickering, Kristen jumped in with a story about her brother. "He is stressed out from all the clutter in his place, but every weekend, he and his wife scour flea markets searching for antiques and bargains. His house, condo, garage, and office overflow with stuff and then he gets stressed out over the debt he's in and how he can never seem to get ahead. And the noodle-noggin doesn't see the connection between how all that spending causes debt, which causes stress, and then all the stuff he spent money on causes clutter, which also causes stress. *Then* they complain that they don't have a life because they both put in overtime hours and are so swamped with so much to do to make extra cash so they can . . . It's just a crazy circle and they don't see the connections between the cause and result."

Sam, a philosopher/salesman, said, "So when we're all stressed out from too much to do, we need to get to the cause—the debt, the spending, and the stuff and clutter. The too-much-spending and the too-much-stuff."

Scott came back with, "Well, who decides how much is too much and how much is enough? Who decides what is a want and what is a need? I think most people aren't at all clear about *why* they are pushing themselves to do more and to always have more. I think most people are stressed out trying to acquire wealth. And who decides what is wealth?"

Sam said, "I don't think 'wealthy' means having a certain amount of money. What amount would that be? I think wealth is based on your need—it means not needing anything else or not much more. The person who is financially broke but grateful he has everything he needs is a wealthy man. When you don't need much more in life, you are truly wealthy. Yet even when people possess more than what seventy percent of what the rest of the world doesn't have, they still feel deprived."

Ask yourself: What is enough? Many people are overworked, overscheduled, and overwhelmed because they are always trying to do more, acquire more. They never question whether they have what they need or have enough.

In order to reduce your stress, you need to do some eliminating and streamlining of the causes of stress—whether it's a packed calendar, too much debt, overwhelming clutter in your life, or whatever.

It also is valuable to question what is enough for kids. Not just in terms of stuff, but activities and other things that might be putting pressure on them. When younger children are asked what makes a family happy, they often come up with the same descriptions:

- Spending time with their parents
- Eating dinner as a family
- Being tucked in at night
- Being read to

They seldom mention computers, cell phones, iPods, money, video games, television, fancy cars, or playing on sports teams.

Shelley and Anita, two airline reservationists, were discussing a gathering of friends who were having a potluck. Everyone was to bring something to contribute to the meal, and Shelley was feeling discouraged. "My calendar is so full," she said, "I have enough time to cook something or come to the potluck, but I can't do both."

Anita replied, "Just bring a container of cottage cheese."

Shelley sputtered, "What? What? What are you talking about?!! I can't show up with just cottage cheese."

Anita countered, "Shell, you know this group. Their self-worth isn't tied in to what they bring to a potluck."

Are you overly busy because your self-worth is tied to what you wear, what you drive, or how your house is decorated? Is it tied to gifts you give or the amount of money you earn? Is it tied to what your business associates think of you or how your friends and family feel about you.? You are in charge of your self-worth—value yourself according to your own values, not someone else's.

One of the best ways to streamline your life is to eliminate letting what other people think rule your life.

Question Everything Before You Commit to It

Where do you start in eliminating or streamlining the "stuff" of your life?

Chip, a video producer, says that he was raised in a house that had a banner hanging in the kitchen that said "Live simply that others may simply live." He says that quote is embedded in his mind and is part of his philosophy of life. It has made it easier for him to ask the types of questions that follow, which cause him to pause and evaluate before plunging into something:

Do I really need to buy this?

Do I have a place to put this?

Do I really need to do this?

Do I really need to own this?

Do I need to join this group?

Do I need to spend my time on this?

Do I really need to have this in my life?

Chip and his family are living a fairly streamlined life according to their values. A few examples are the family members drive an older car, give deliberate thought to purchases so there is very little impulse buying, and don't use charge cards, and everyone in the family has agreed to not pay big bucks for the "privilege of having designer names on anything." In other words, if a designer something is a good value, they buy it. If it is similar to something else but the price is quadrupled because it has a designer name on it, then they don't buy it.

In exchange for a simplified lifestyle, his wife is able to work part-time instead of full-time, and Chip does not have to accept overtime hours at work. They are still able to treat themselves to fun family activities throughout the year.

Chip says that nobody ever said on their deathbed, "I wish I'd spent more time at the office." And he and his wife are determined to not have regrets about missing out on their children's growing-up years. For their family, eliminating and streamlining means cutting back on cash investments, which in turn cuts down on the need to work overly long hours. For others, it means having a choice about how time is spent, money is earned, or other areas of their lives.

Sometimes people wonder whether if they start to say no to things that once were important—for the sake of simplifying their lives and preventing stress—they'll be messing up the life values we read about earlier. First, let's explore the difference between priorities and values. When you work on priorities, you decide "This task comes first, next I have to do that."

Values reflect what is important in your life, what is valuable to you. Is it health? Your relationship with God? Family? Friends? Love? Music? Justice? Art? Freedom? Helping others? Saving the whales? Combating global warming? Teaching others? Making the world a better place?

Once values are clarified, you can brainstorm ways to incorporate them in your life. When you know you value time alone or time with family or friends, you can focus on ways to simplify your schedule or calendar.

If you value travel or a vacation, you can focus on simplifying your needs and expenditures. In exchange for taking a fun family vacation every year, one family decided to forgo a DVD player, second computer, and sophisticated cell phone plan, and to put strict limits on eating fast food and buying expensive coffee. They arranged for others to take care of the dad's mother who was confined to the house. The family returned from vacation each year with renewed energy for taking care of the incapacitated grandmother.

When you live life spending more time on what is not important to you and little or no time on what is truly important to you, the result is usually stress, frustration, and a sense of inadequacy.

The Excess of Success

What do you think success is? What is your definition of success as a person, spouse, parent, worker, wage earner, or member of an organization, team, or church?

When author and actor Malachy McCourt was asked his thoughts on streamlining our lives, he said, "We are born with a wheelbarrow to help us carry through our lives whatever we need. But many people keep asking for—and getting—bigger and bigger wheelbarrows.

"Some of them hit a point that it will topple over or they can't push it anymore so they collapse right in the middle of the wheelbarrow road.

"Others just keep piling stuff higher and higher, and never realize they are heading for the edge of a cliff. And of course the stuff goes over the cliff with them, but you still can't take it with you. The moral of the story is you can't give or receive the gifts of life with hands on the handles of an overloaded wheelbarrow."

Use a Time Log to Eliminate and Streamline

Many people hate the idea of a time log, but that might be because it forces them to face reality. Listing in a log or a journal all the ways you spend your time might leave you feeling embarrassed to admit you waste a lot of time or you are spending most of your time on things you least value.

You don't have to keep a time log forever. One week will give you fabulous insights. Even logging your activities for just a day or two will help you see where you can start to eliminate or streamline activities.

Kevin, a CEO, said that his best time management tip was learning to say no. The first time he ever kept a time log (and he says every once in a while he goes back to keeping one) he realized that he was putting everyone else's priorities and urgent matters before his own. He was on "commitment overload," making too many appointments, taking on too many relationships and too many responsibilities, volunteering for too many tasks, serving on too many committees. He was trying to be all things to everyone.

When he asked himself why he was involved in a particular organization, he had to admit he was simply living up to his own expectation and there was no real reason to belong to it. It took him a long time to grasp that just because you *can* do something doesn't mean you *have* to.

Kevin cut back everywhere, and not only in those areas that caused him stress. "What I had been doing was saying yes to everything that sounded like fun," he said. "And I was surprised to discover that doing many, many fun activities all at once leaves me exhausted and stressed out. Now I've learned my best way to eliminate and streamline is to say no frequently."

Control Clutter to Lessen Stress

Clutter in your life keeps you busy. You've got to find space for it, maintain it, clean it or clean around it, insure it, protect it. The fewer things you have surrounding you, the easier it is to keep your living and working space neat and clean. Also, when you have clutter in your work space or living space, you have clutter in your mind and in your heart; you can't think clearly and don't know what you feel.

Have you ever noticed how clutter sucks the energy out of the marrow of your bones? Just looking at all that stuff and thinking about clearing it out can be so exhausting that you want to take a nap. Another benefit to clutter busting is that once the stuff you don't need or use is gone, you can finally find things when you search for them.

Once clutter is diminished, you will feel more energized and experience the overwhelming desire to dance the dance of joy all over town. Plus it will be easier to focus on what you need to and want to do.

Eliminate and Streamline Information and Paper

Regarding information overload, Richard A. Swenson, M.D., wrote in *Margin: Restoring Emotional, Physical, Financial, and Time*

Reserves to Overloaded Lives, "A single edition of the *New York Times* contains more information than a seventeenth-century Britisher would encounter in a lifetime."

It is no longer possible to read or absorb all the information coming your way. You need new methods for going through your mail and e-mail and handling all the reading material that is gushing into your life like a never-ending waterfall.

Skim through mail, e-mail, books, and newsletters. Cancel subscriptions to all those magazines stacking up in the corner that you plan to read someday but never find the time for. Recycle catalogs without looking through them. Better yet, go online to www .catalogchoice.org, a free service that lets you decline paper catalogs you no longer wish to receive. You will reduce the amount of unsolicited mail in your mailbox while helping to preserve the environment. But when catalogs you choose to receive start to pile up, just tell yourself there is nothing in there that is important enough to add to your clutter.

Be highly selective when downloading or printing reams of material from Web sites. They may contain important information but nobody has time to read all of them. Skim them, pausing to carefully read or print out only those parts that seem to be new, fresh, important, or extremely interesting.

Create Time-Saving Systems for Dealing with Information and Paper

Develop systems for handling information or tasks that keep coming up again and again. If people routinely ask for certain information, set up a self-help section at work or on the server where colleagues can access it. Write out all the steps and hand them the paper or send them to a Web site, instead of wasting your time on the phone explaining the same steps to everyone.

Organize your own electronic and paper files so you can quickly find the answers to questions you are often asked. Notice what kinds of queries exasperate you because you have to run around looking for the answers—this is a tip-off that you need to reorganize your files to make retrieval of information more automatic and less stressful.

If your kids aren't getting their chores done or need to be reminded of what to do to get ready for school, write out the steps and post your list where the kids can see it. For children who are too young to read, cut out pictures from magazines of a child brushing her teeth or getting dressed or eating breakfast. Let your child help with the list; the more involved they are with it, the more likely they will be to follow it.

If you are sending out repetitive letters or e-mails, make up templates or form letters. Or create FAQ (Frequently Asked Questions) sheets for co-workers, clients, customers, volunteers, patients, even family.

If your computer or PDA has a way of giving you reminders (most computers do), learn how to work them. Some computers have reminders that blink, flash, ding, and practically tap you on the shoulder and hand you a cup of coffee. Once you start using these reminders to help keep you on top of your list of things to do, you'll wonder how you were able to function without them.

Outsource Certain Tasks

Businesses outsource work all the time. Is there anything in your life you can outsource or at least ask for help with?

Bill was in charge of mowing the lawn and often let it go for so long that the grass was above the height of his kids' knees. This made his wife, Jane, crazy and they had huge arguments over it. He claimed he only put it off because he was busy; she claimed he'd better change his priorities about what is important to do around the house.

A friend gave Jane the contact information for a lawn mowing company. She was astonished to discover it cost less to pay people to cut their grass than it cost to buy dinner for the family once a week. Years later, she still refers to the lawn company as the wonderful guys who saved her marriage.

Maybe you can't afford to have someone clean your house every week, but it's a great stress buster when you are under extreme pressure during the holidays, when you have overnight company, or when your mother-in-law is coming to dinner. Saving your sanity may be worth the cost of a cleaning service.

Whether you consider the help frequently or on rare occasions, sometimes you can eliminate a great deal of stress by paying someone to wash your car, help with the children, cook a meal, clean up after a party, stay with your invalid father, or a hundred and one other stresses when you find yourself running on that hamster wheel.

Schedule Streamlining Days

Myron, executive director of a landscaping association, has an interesting system. "I have days I streamline everything I can; those are my days devoted to catching up. My e-mail replies are one or two words, I scroll through and eliminate every e-mail I can, I set a timer for five minutes for all my phone calls (unless absolutely impossible), zip through any snail mail that has stacked up, and any magazines or catalogs I haven't read since my last streamline day get tossed into the recycle bin.

"I noticed that a momentum or a mood comes over me, so as long as I'm in my 'eliminating mode,' I check my closets, even the kitchen cabinets. You know, when you put yourself in a mood to get rid of and reduce papers at your desk, it can carry over to your whole house. On those days, I fill up dozens of bags of stuff to donate to the Vietnam vets organization."

Most of us cannot devote a whole day to scaling back our work, but we can do any of a number of variations on Myron's ideas.

Dave, who works out of his home, has a "power hour" at least once a week where he powers through his e-mails—deleting them, sending short replies, or making a decision and handling the complicated ones he put aside earlier and then forgot about.

Melody is a teacher who collects all kinds of craft items and articles with ideas for her classroom. Every year, the week after school ends, she has a "zip morning." She zips through all that she has accumulated and either tosses out, recycles, or files it. She used to be terrified of throwing away something she might need next year, but she finally realized that stuff comes into her life as if she was a magnet and will turn into overwhelming clutter if she doesn't clear it out once a year.

After she gets rid of almost everything at the end of the school year, she somehow collects a whole new batch of articles and craft supplies even before the next school year begins. "Now," Mel says, "I zip through everything and zip most of it out the door."

Gayle says every spring her mother had the whole family go through the house and clear out what they no longer needed or used. Now Gayle does it with her family. She cleans out closets and cabinets, her husband goes through the garage getting rid of things, and the kids clear out their toys and clothes. It's a spring ritual that works for her family.

Some people simply develop a habit of going through their clutter or stacks of paper every day and either putting things where they belong or getting rid of them. It doesn't matter whether you schedule a few minutes or a full day to streamline. If you do not regularly schedule *any* time for it, you will find yourself feeling overwhelmed and stressed.

Look for Creative Alternatives

You can radically reduce your stress by eliminating the negative attached to so many life events. It's almost expected that we get depressed over certain birthdays, hate Monday mornings because we are returning to work, and dread getting together with the family at holidays. What can you do to turn around a negative event or eliminate the negative aspects of it—especially if you can't change the event?

Katie and her three friends discussed that there was nothing they could do to prevent their upcoming fiftieth birthdays, so instead of being depressed over that milestone, they decided to create a positive. They all felt they needed to step out of their comfort circle and go on an adventure. They decided to drive from their home in Chicago to Colorado to go river rafting, because they felt that getting smacked in the face with icy cold water and navigating terrifying rapids would fill them with the exhilaration of life.

As they left Chicago, they discovered that for each of them, it was their first vacation without their children, so they made up some fun rules. Whoever sat in the backseat had to whine: "Are we almost there yet?" "Her foot's on my side." "How much longer till we get there?" "Make her stop looking at me!" Then someone would count to three and they'd all whine, "I have to go to the baaaaaaathroom." Another rule was whoever sat behind the driver had to kick the back of the seat for hours.

After their rafting adventure, Katie described feeling like a returning hero as she pulled into the driveway and roared into the house, excited to tell her twenty-one-year-old son, Jeff, all about her trip. He had been home alone for the ten days of her trip, and when Katie went into the house she stopped dead in her tracks. The house was immaculately clean. (Wouldn't that make you nervous?) She looked around and said to Jeff, "Wow, even the dishes are clean!"

Jeff said, "You know when a guy knows it's time to do the dishes?"

Katie said no, and Jeff, ever the comedian, said, "When he's eating his Froot Loops out of a bundt cake pan with an ice cream scoop."

So Katie and her friends, instead of living up to the world's expectation that they would be depressed over their fiftieth, spent a year saving for and planning their high adventure, and now they have great stories to tell. If you can't change the situation itself, then see if you can do something to eliminate the negative and add a positive note to it.

What about people who are taking care of elderly parents, young children, or chronically ill people? How can they streamline?

For some people, even a time log shows that there is nothing that can be omitted in their packed schedule. For example, a single mom working two or three jobs cannot opt to work fewer hours in order to reduce her stress—or outsource chores so she has more time to relax.

Still, there may be some alternatives. Whitney, a bagger at a grocery store who also cleans houses on her days off, is a single mom who found a very creative solution. The woman upstairs who also had daughters and who worked nights had become a close friend.

The two women decided to move in together, and because they worked opposite hours, they each could babysit when the other one was working. They saved the cost of child care and eased a lot of stress knowing their children were with a safe, loving, reliable woman. They were a bit crowded, but all were willing to put up with the crowded conditions because of the financial benefits, and it was wonderful having two women share the cooking and cleaning. Such a solution is not suitable for everyone, but it has worked for Whitney for several years.

A DO-NOT-DO LIST

Just as a to-do list helps you focus on what you need to do, a do-not-do list can help you stop doing what you don't need to do. Here are a few ideas to get you started:

DO NOT

- compare yourself to others
- believe you have to work to the point of exhaustion to be considered a capable person
- try to please everybody you know
- spend your time acting on everybody else's priorities
- say yes to every request
- think that being busy is a standard of success
- consider it necessary to take care of every single person you know in order to be liked
- believe that you never have time for your priorities
- hang on to angers and resentments
- try to live up to the expectations of everyone in the world (including you)
- strive to be so independent you never need (or are able) to ask for help from others
- spend time on busywork that's not important to you

Avoid Multifocusing When You
Think You're Multitasking

If you have read or heard anyone discuss multitasking, you know what the advice is.

Do it.

Don't do it.

Maybe sometimes do it.

Under the right circumstances, do it.

It's helpful, not helpful, effective, ineffective, it's right, it's wrong, it's good, it's bad.

The funny thing is, when people are telling you how wrong it is to multitask, they often are telling you while opening mail, logging on to a computer, or folding laundry. The frustrating part is that there are so many definitions and styles of multitasking that when two people discuss it, they often are discussing two totally different activities.

When you are doing two tasks at the same time, you are dividing your thinking, focus, attention, and concentration between two activities. If both tasks call for high thought or focus, neither will be done well. Typing an important e-mail while listening to an important phone call can result in your missing some key details on the phone and sending out a garbled, incorrect, or incomplete e-mail. This is not smart multitasking.

Many people extend "multitasking" to mean working on three different projects in one hour and not completing any of them. If you are doing that because you cannot stay focused on one task for a long period of time or you were forced to stop each task for a reason, then you're doing fine. No problem. But if your idea of multitasking is simply to bounce from one project to another and kid yourself that you are doing three things at once, think again. Each time you start a new task, you have stopped the old one. You are not doing three things at once; you are multifocusing. You are starting and stopping; you lose focus and you lose the precious time it takes trying to wonder, "Now where was I and what was I going to do next?"

Multifocusing your way through several projects at the same time ensures that you will feel pressured and stressed. Each task is not accomplished as well as it could be. The work on each is so fragmented that you lack the deep pleasure that comes with a job well done. You don't have the satisfaction of completing one task to help motivate you to do the next. And you might miss a deadline or drop the ball on important stuff while switching your focus from one project to another. Also you lose momentum when you interrupt good concentration and never allow yourself to move into "the zone."

When something is important and deserves your full attention and concentration, then develop the habit of putting everything aside and giving it the focus it deserves. Doing this one task and completing it will enable you to do it well.

And what about those tasks that do not need your full attention or concentration? Go ahead and multitask. As long as you aren't trying to divide your focus in half, you are doing smart multitasking. When you have one task that needs very little concentration, then you are able to give plenty of thought and focus to the other task. Some examples of smart multitasking are:

- planning a grocery list while loading the dishwasher
- making a phone call while printing out a two-hundred-page report
- exercising while you listen to marketing CDs
- paying bills while doing the laundry
- assembling promotional packets while brainstorming marketing ideas

It's not the multitasking that creates stress, it's the multifocusing that gets us into trouble and leaves us frazzled.

Raiman was conscientious about answering his phone as soon as it rang and checking his e-mail as soon as he heard the "you've got mail" announcement. But he realized that putting this expectation on himself was resulting in constant interruptions. He found that by turning off his phone and checking his e-mail only once or twice a day he dramatically increased his productivity. Raiman said that he has been surprised to read that many successful CEOs and other high achievers frequently turn off phones and e-mail for long periods of time when they need uninterrupted hours for thinking or creative work.

Thoughts to Ponder

Out of abundance He took abundance and still
abundance remains.

— the Upanishads

Joy is what happens to us when we allow ourselves to recognize how good things really are.

—MARIANNE WILLIAMSON

The truth is, the happy get happier because they know how to be happy, and the troubled get more troubled because they pour all their energy into their troubles.

—SUSAN PAGE

He who knows enough is enough will always have enough.

—LAO-TZU

Until you make peace with who you are, you'll never be content with what you have.

—DORIS MORTMAN

You will recognize your own path when you come upon it, because you will suddenly have all the energy and imagination you will ever need.

—JERRY GILLIES

Few things are necessary to make the wise man happy, while no amount of material wealth would satisfy a fool. I am not a fool.

—OG MANDINO

Being rich isn't about money. Being rich is a state of mind. Some of us, no matter how much money we have, will never be free enough to take time to stop and eat the heart of the watermelon. And some of us will be rich without ever being more than a paycheck ahead of the game.

—Harvey Mackay

And there is no greatness where there is not simplicity, goodness and truth.

—Leo Tolstoy

If your outgo exceeds your income, your upkeep will be your downfall.

—Anonymous

To earn the appreciation of honest critics and endure the betrayal of false friends; to appreciate beauty; to find the best in others; to leave the world a bit better, whether by a healthy child, a garden patch, or a redeemed social condition; to know even one life has breathed easier because you lived. This is to have succeeded.

—Ralph Waldo Emerson

Simplify your life. You do not need all the clutter you are holding on to. Get rid of it now. Keep around you only the things that give you energy.

—John-Roger

Year by year the complexities of this spinning world grow more bewildering and so each year we need all the

more to seek peace and comfort in the joyful
simplicities.

—*WOMAN'S HOME COMPANION*, 1935

'Tis a gift to be simple,
'Tis a gift to be free,
'Tis a gift to come down
Where we ought to be
And when we find ourselves
In the place that's right
'Twill be in the valley
of love and delight.

—NINETEENTH-CENTURY SHAKER HYMN

He threw himself on his horse and rode off in all
directions.

—MIGUEL DE CERVANTES, *DON QUIXOTE*

Success is having what you want
Happiness is wanting what you have

—ANONYMOUS

Think no other greatness but that of the soul, no other
riches but those of the heart.

—JOHN QUINCY ADAMS

Our remedies oft in ourselves do lie
—WILLIAM SHAKESPEARE, *ALL'S WELL THAT ENDS WELL*

Success isn't permanent, and failure isn't fatal.
—MIKE DITKA

What I am is good enough, if I would only be it openly
—CARL ROGERS

EXTRA CREDIT

1. When you spot yourself feeling overly busy, overscheduled, and overwhelmed, stop and ask: Why are you so busy? If your answer is, "That's how my life is," then question it even further. *Why* is that how your life is?
2. Do you believe you have to be exhausted to be successful?
3. Do you think you have to be exhausted to achieve your dreams?
4. What's the first thing you thought of when you read the chapter title "Eliminate What You Can and Streamline Everything Else"?

_____

_____

_____

5. After giving it some thought, where do you think you need to do some eliminating and streamlining?

_____

_____

_____

6. What would be your biggest obstacle to doing that eliminating and streamlining?

_____

_____

_____

7. What are the first steps you can take to get started?

_____

_____

_____

CHAPTER 6

Set Boundaries at Work and at Home

SETTING BOUNDARIES IN YOUR LIFE CAN go a long way toward helping you manage your time and reduce your stress.

During a particularly difficult fourteen days of work, Traci realized she had only one evening off—the upcoming Saturday. So when her evening off arrived, she decided to cut off all connections with the outside world and catch up on laundry, relax, pet her cat, and watch every episode of *Law & Order* she could find.

Just as she was heading over to turn off her phone, it rang. Her sister called to tell her they needed a fourth person for their bridge game. She enthusiastically told Traci how much fun it would be if she joined them and what a rotten, boring evening it would be for them if Traci didn't come over.

Traci explained her exhausting workload and said she really needed to stay home on this very precious evening off. Her sister didn't buy it. She whined. She begged. She pleaded. Then she told Traci how selfish she was to ruin their bridge game.

Notice the guilt and manipulation her sister was using. She

wanted Traci to be responsible for the happiness or sadness of the three bridge players. Why can't they find someone else? Why can't they do something else? Oh, no, it's up to Traci to come and save their happy evening.

Boundaries define where things begin and end, but it seems there's always someone out there disagreeing with that boundary and wanting to either cross it or change it. Traci learned a lot from this experience. She learned that others might not respect her boundaries, but it's important that she respect them and respect herself and her own needs and priorities. She also learned to use her voice mail and not return calls on a night when she has decided to curl up and simply be alone and cozy.

Maura firmly believes it is important to volunteer time for children and she loved being a Cub Scout leader. So she couldn't figure out why she was reluctant to agree to her friend Sharon's request to be treasurer of the parents' club.

Sometime later there was an emergency in Maura's extended family. Her sister-in-law was sick from chemotherapy, so Maura called a few family members to coordinate ways people could help out. Her aunt said, "Please don't ask me to cook or take care of the kids, but I'd be happy to put on my sweats and come over and clean her house. I'd even enjoy doing her windows."

Maura was relieved because she hated house cleaning and window washing but actually enjoyed taking care of her sister-in-law's children. In that instant, Maura realized why she had said no to being club treasurer. She would have been miserable doing the administrative task. From then on, Maura decided to set boundaries on her volunteer work and accept only jobs she likes and that suit her interests and abilities—only jobs that light her up.

Eleven Tips for Setting Boundaries That Lessen Your Stress

In today's world, constant access to work—phones, computers, BlackBerries, and PDAs—controls our lives, even at the dinner table or in a restaurant. *We need boundaries* for when, where, how, and for how long we will hand over control of our lives to outside demands. Here are eleven tested strategies for managing your time at work, at home, and doing volunteer work; for establishing a healthy balance between your priorities and those of others; and for achieving your goals without working yourself to death or alienating your family and friends.

Having a desk or office in the home blurs the line of demarcation between work and home life even more.

We need boundaries between work time and personal time.

We look at our schedule and feel exhausted by all that we have to do and all the places we have to go.

We need boundaries on our schedules.

Our boundaries might cover:

- what we do (I'll do this but not that)
- where we do it (I'll do this at work but not at home)
- how long we do it (I'll take over this job for a month but if you don't have a replacement by then, I have to remove myself from the committee)

If you are serious about reducing your stress, you must learn about and start to set boundaries in your life.

1. Know When to Cry "Uncle"

Mary Ann knows she can get so wrapped up in pursuing a goal that she can become obsessive. It's a good trait when the goal is important, but she can get obsessed over the craziest, most insignificant pursuits. Mary Ann said she really needed to learn "when to stop beating my head against the wall."

Once she offered to find some information for her daughter's scout leader. She thought it would involve a phone call or two, but instead she ended up spending three days on the phone, with pages of notes and a list of things to follow up on. The stress of tracking down information, making and receiving calls, keeping everything straight, and making lists was giving her a headache that would not stop.

As we talked about boundaries, she said she hated the idea of telling the scout leader that she wasn't successful in her "mission." But as she thought about it, she realized she had to become selective. Her persistence is a great habit for something important, but to obsess over every single search is not a good use of her time.

Now Mary Ann sets boundaries for herself. If she takes on a quest, she decides beforehand how much time, energy, and attention she will devote to that project. And then she forces herself to stop.

If it relates to work and they need whatever it is Mary Ann is searching for, of course she will continue till she finds what she needs. But that is not where she usually gets into a high-stress frazzle. Her high-stress situations almost always involve noncritical, volunteer tasks. And she has learned that they often turn into wild-goose chases.

2. KEEP WORK TIME AND FAMILY TIME SEPARATE

Jason, a publicist, works out of his home office and was battling several stress-related illnesses. He would answer the phone during dinner, start developing a marketing campaign, and still be working on it well past midnight.

His wife and children became so resentful of his putting work before them that they hardly spoke to him. Jason felt the chill in the family but believed there was nothing else he could do. He felt that was the only way to run a successful business.

One day he heard a ruckus in the house and came out of his office to discover a celebration going on. His daughter's softball team had won the championship. And even though she was beaming with pride holding her trophy, she walked right past him and didn't bother to show it to him.

In that instant, Jason realized he not only had forgotten about the championship games, he was totally out of touch with his whole family. He had treated them as if they didn't matter, and now he didn't matter enough to his daughter for her to even show him her trophy.

Finally, he decided to set boundaries such as no interruptions during family time, and that included turning off his cell phone. This was painful at first but eventually he learned that life goes on and his business will succeed without the constant ringing of a cell phone. As he started to set boundaries and honor them, his health, his family dynamics, and his whole life began to turn around.

3. BE CREATIVE WHEN WORK MUST INTERRUPT PERSONAL TIME

Sometimes work has to interrupt family time, such as when an obstetrician receives a call in the midst of a family celebration and is told he's needed in the delivery room. He has to head for the hospital regardless of how disappointed his children are.

Marge, a neonatal nurse in Illinois, reports that some doctors have found ways to blend work and family. "One night one of our best doctors brought her adorable four-year-old daughter, Ally, with her to the hospital to check on a patient," Marge said. "The nurses were happy to see Ally and chat with her in the nurses' station and she got to be with her mom at work. The doc was only there for ten minutes, but if you count the ride in and out, the doc probably spent at least an extra hour with her child. Even the chief of obstetrics has brought her teenage daughter Colleen on the unit while she was taking care of some paperwork for a few minutes. Recently, a doctor came in wearing her soccer mom shirt to do surgery, then returned to her kid's game."

Often it takes only a bit of creative problem-solving to change having to work on your day off into a pleasant, fun experience.

Michael, a meeting planner for a major restaurant chain, is the single father of five-year-old Nadia and is very protective of his time off work. He doesn't use his cell phone away from work and takes no work-related phone calls or e-mails at home, although every so often, he might use his laptop to write a proposal after Nadia is asleep.

Occasionally people for whom he has planned a meeting insist that he be there in person on a Sunday, his day off. Sundays are very important to Michael and Nadia, so when a customer insists on Michael showing up for a Sunday event, he and Nadia both dress up and go to the restaurant together. Michael stops in at the meeting he planned, then he and his daughter have lunch together.

They have a special meal out and the customer is happy. Michael picked up this way of setting a boundary from his boss, Norma, who follows the same system, except if she has to come to a meeting on her day off, she invites a friend to join her for lunch or dinner after she makes an appearance at the meeting. Both meeting planners have a clear determination to protect their personal time and they both make every effort to guard that boundary.

4. Say No to Some Commitments

Lisa is a professional speaker whose generosity caused her great stress and lost her a huge amount of money. She had the habit of saying yes to every request for her to speak free of charge to organizations in her town, and she did a great job. She also received requests from branches of the same organizations in other towns. Lisa spoke free of charge as often as three times a week. As a result, she sometimes turned down paying jobs because she was already booked at a local church, school, or organization.

Worse than that, Lisa found herself on the brink of exhaustion and totally stressed out from all the talks she was giving. Since she makes her living as a speaker, she had the additional stress of money concerns and worried that she couldn't pay her bills.

Finally, Lisa learned to put a boundary on her free talks. One a month, that's it.

Being generous is wonderful, but if it leaves you sick, exhausted, and not able to pay the mortgage, then something is wrong. It's no longer generosity. It's just plain dumb. Those people in her audience don't go to work and say "Hey, skip the paycheck this week. I'll work for free." Why do they expect Lisa to do it? Setting boundaries has allowed Lisa to present some talks free of charge without having to be the free speaker for every organization in her state.

Eddy, a contractor, says that he and his wife have been trying to cut back on all their commitments because they are both exhausted and stressed to the max with a schedule of trying to take care of everyone's needs and attend every activity they are invited to. They *know* what they need to do. They just don't know how to do it.

"When a neighbor asks me to come and help him with a plumbing problem, I might be tired and I might need to fix something at our house, but I know how to fix this type of thing and he doesn't, so I say yes . . . because I don't know how to say no.

"And my wife is the same way. When someone asks her to do something or go somewhere, she might not want to do it, but she just doesn't know what to say."

One day it hit Eddy that he's not the only one who can help people. If he was out of town, his neighbors and friends would have to figure out a different way to solve their problems. He decided he will occasionally give them help (that's a boundary!) but not every time they ask.

He and his wife have come to the realization that they can't keep treating everybody's commitments as more important than their own. By figuring that out, their journey of stress busting is half-complete. The second half is learning what to say in order to set boundaries, believing you have the right to say no, and saying it with strength and conviction.

What to Say When You Want to Say No but People Really Want to Hear Yes

"Usually I can work on your committee, but not this time. I've just got too much going."

"I'd love to do that but not at this time in my life."

"I would like to do that but I have way too many commitments right now and cannot possibly squeeze this in."

"You know, that would be fun, but I simply can't."

"I'd love to help with your project at work, but I too have priorities and if I do yours, I'll never get mine done."

"I'd really like to come over to help you with your plumbing problem, but I'm tied up tonight and I just can't. I'm sorry."

"Thank you for asking me. I'm honored and glad you asked; unfortunately I can't serve as president of the board this year."

"Dang! I've always wanted to do that, but this isn't the right time for me. Thank you for asking."

"Under normal circumstances, I would be more than happy to oblige you, but things are a bit crazy right now and I can't do it."

"I would love to do that. What day did you say it was? Sorry, I can't make it. I have plans." (The person asking you probably will not think your plans are as important as his request, so don't explain the plans. Just say you have 'em.)

5. PLACE TIME LIMITS ON PHONE CALLS

If others do not respect the value of your time, it's up to you to set limits and enforce them.

Sue, the mother of two children under two years of age, said her sister-in-law Charlotte was making her crazy. When Charlotte was bored, she would pop in on Sue unexpectedly or call her for long phone conversations. Then she would talk about the same problems over and over but wasn't ever willing to do anything to solve them.

One evening, Sue complained to her husband, "Doesn't she realize that with taking care of two babies, I don't have all that time to give her?"

He replied, "Well, either she doesn't realize it, or she does but doesn't care." In that instant, Sue decided to put boundaries on Charlotte.

Now, when Charlotte calls, Sue tells her right up front, "I'm swamped today, so we only have ten minutes to chat." Then she sets a timer. When it dings, Charlotte is never ready to hang up. Sometimes she manipulatively starts to talk about a problem or about feeling depressed, so Sue very assertively says, "I'm so sorry, but the kids need me and I've gotta go now. Let's finish this another time."

When Charlotte drops by unannounced Sue reminds her that she needs to let her know when she wants to come over because sometimes, "like today," there are a million things to do.

As Charlotte settles down at the kitchen table to have a cup of coffee, Sue invites her to join her in the basement as she does the laundry. One time, Charlotte dropped in and Sue was all caught up on laundry, so Sue started cleaning out her cabinets.

She is determined to set boundaries on her sister-in-law. She feels proud of herself for reminding Charlotte to call before visiting and feels very satisfied that she's gotten Charlotte to join her in doing chores. And now that her stress has eased up, she finds herself starting to like Charlotte a lot more.

6. SET REALISTICALLY REACHABLE GOALS

If you feel that you are working as hard as you possibly can but are never getting ahead or accomplishing what you want to, that can become one of your biggest sources of stress.

Henry, a business/technology consultant, says that much of the stress of managers in the corporate world is self-inflicted: "The stress occurs when expectations of accomplishment exceed ability to deliver. Ironically, most of the unattainable expectations are set by the manager himself. In not clearly understanding their own goals, they fall into 'fire-fighting' mode. All unexpected challenges are treated as crises. They are each addressed immediately with all resources available."

Staff is constantly asked to drop what they're doing to focus on the new problem, yet they never actually fix the problem. There is only time for temporary solutions before the next crisis.

He suggests that managers need to stop going from one crisis to another. Instead, when a problem arises, they should run a root cause analysis. "An example of a root cause," says Henry, "would be a software bug that eventually eats all available memory until a system crashes. To fix it, a major section of the code needs to be rewritten. Everybody knows this. But it will take time. And during that time, customers are complaining. So, rather then rewrite the code, it is decided that they will substantially increase the system's memory.

"The problem still exists and will reoccur, but not for a while. The customers no longer complain, but everyone involved knows, at the back of their minds, this issue isn't really off their plate. The manager knows they have worked long and hard, but also knows that none of these problems have been put to rest. But what can he do? He obviously doesn't have the people to address the root causes of problems at the moment. Everyone is too busy.

"The answer is not a technology fix; they must put a boundary on the time they are spending putting out fires. The manager needs to clearly state the nature of the problem to management (a memory leak), and sell them on the need for a long-term solution. Then it needs to be clearly explained to the customers that this is going to take some time to fix, but once it is, it will stay fixed." It's better to work on solving the problem than to continue to rely on superficial or temporary fixes. Not only will customers' satisfaction increase, there will be less overtime pay, and managers and staff will be less overworked and frustrated.

7. LIMIT PHONE INTERRUPTIONS

Deborah was working on an extremely important presentation she was giving the next morning to the company's newest customer. She felt that doing a great job could be important for her career.

The phone rang. It was a friend who had recently experienced a tragic, devastating loss. The friend was in tears. Deborah was painfully aware that this exact same phone conversation had occurred about ten days earlier. At that time, Deb sat listening and weeping with her friend for more than an hour. Deb was working on another presentation then also, and after the phone call, it had taken her till past midnight to wrap it up. When she woke up the next morning at five thirty, her usual time, she was sluggish and felt as if she were drugged. Her stress level soared as she walked in to do the program, and she wished she felt more prepared and therefore more confident. The client's response was OK, not great. Deborah had a seriously upset stomach for three days.

Now she was being given a second chance to make another presentation. And here she was with the same friend in need on the phone. As much as she loved her friend and her heart ached for her friend's sorrow, Deborah knew she could not stay on this phone call or it might mean the end of (or at least a downturn in) her career. Besides, she couldn't take the stress of another late-night session and walking into a presentation scared and unconfident.

She said, "You know I love you and care about you and I really want to spend time with you. But I'm distracted working on a really important presentation for tomorrow. Can I call you when I get home from work and then I can give you my full attention? I would be just so distracted right now."

Her friend's reaction astonished her. Instead of sounding disappointed, her friend asked about the presentation. She said she'd love Deborah to call her the next day so she could hear all about how everything went and promised to pray for Deborah the next morning during her "big gig." Deborah told her how grateful she was, and the conversation ended on a positive note.

What Deborah said was perfect. After all, wouldn't anyone prefer to talk to us when we can give our full attention instead of at a time we admit to being distracted? She started to use this same phrase when her teenagers interrupted her while preparing for important meetings. She would say, "I'm really distracted right now. Can we talk about this in about an hour when I can give you my full attention and be fully present to you?"

The girls have even started to use that phrase themselves. Recently, her eldest daughter told her, "Mom, I have so much on my mind right now, I know what you mean about being present or not. My body is here but my mind is a million miles away. Can we cover this later?"

So Deborah has not only learned to set boundaries and prevent high levels of stress, she has also taught the skill to her daughters.

8. CUT BACK ON SOME FAMILY TRADITIONS

When you find yourself stressed from all that you have to do, stop and see whose expectations you are living up to. Charmaine tells the story of being behind schedule in putting up Christmas decorations one year. Instead of spreading out the work over several days as they usually did, she pushed to get everything up in one day. She was determined to make the house beautiful for her family.

They pulled out all the boxes of decorations, hauled them up from the basement, put up the tree, put the ornaments and lights on the tree (at this point, tempers were flaring and everyone was cranky), and continued putting up the garland, lights, and other decorations all over the house. Everyone was stressed and exhausted.

As her thirteen-year-old daughter stomped off to bed, she said, "Mom, I hope you know we only did this because you wanted it. I don't give a darn about all the stupid decorations."

Charmaine was startled and chalked it up to her daughter being in a bad mood. But as she gave more thought to it, she realized that much of her stress during the holidays came from her struggle to live up to her own expectations. That year she decided to cut way down on baking. Nobody complained. Nobody noticed or cared. And Charmaine saved hours and hours of time and work by not going into her customary baking frenzy. Now each year she limits what she expects of herself (and her family) during the holiday.

Another way to put boundaries on expectations is to first find out if you have a clear idea of what is expected of you. Otherwise you might be agreeing (or refusing to agree) to expectations that don't even exist.

Victoria told a story about her grandparents. They came to the U.S. from Austria as newlyweds, and every Saturday morning Grandmother made homemade raisin coffee cake for Victoria's grandfather to give him a taste of home. After twenty-six years of marriage, Grandmother discovered that her husband hated raisins. "So why didn't you tell me? Don't you think I have better things to do than to bake you a coffee cake that you hate?" she asked him.

"I thought you were supposed to make it and I was expected to eat it to make you happy."

Epilogue: She stopped baking every Saturday morning and instead joined a water aerobics class.

9. Enlist Your Boss's Help Managing an Overwhelming Workload

If on your job you have more than one person feeding work to your desk or if you have a boss who is fairly oblivious about how swamped you are, you have to set a boundary.

Most bosses really don't know how much work you have or how long something takes. So often they will say, "Here, can you do this? It shouldn't take you long." Yet a week later you are still buried under the burden of that task.

The place to start is to make a list of all your top-priority work and take it in to the boss or e-mail it. Say something like "As you can see, this all cannot possibly be done today, and I've been staying late to get work done, but today I need to leave when everyone else does. Can you advise me on what's most important for me to complete today?"

Usually that works. Sometimes it doesn't. Pearl said something similar to her boss and he blew her off. He said, "It's your job to get it all done. That's what you get paid for."

She asked if perhaps there was someone who could work with her on a few of the projects and was discouraged when he said there wasn't. But later Pearl noticed a definite improvement in her workload. Her boss was passing some of the work on to other staff members and a week later he asked Pearl if she was still having to stay past five o'clock.

She was touched by his concern and delighted that she was able to cut way back on staying late and to go home at five.

10. CUT BACK ON YOUR CHILD'S SCHEDULE

Brendan and his family kept a crazy schedule. They never had dinner together. Actually, the only thing they did together was drive the kids to and from activities, and usually it was him taking one child one way and his wife with another child heading off in a different direction.

He was becoming more aware of how the franticness caused stress for him and his wife, and also he was spotting signs of stress in each of their four children, including sleep disturbance, a drop in grades, and a lot of squabbling going on. They had a family meeting and Brendan pointed out that they *had* to set some boundaries in their lifestyle. He told the children that each of them needed to eliminate and streamline some of their activities. Three of the four seemed almost relieved and were willing to drop down to one activity each. One child squawked a bit, but eventually worked her activities down to basketball and flute.

Suddenly, life became manageable and the stress level in the family lowered.

As part of the boundary-setting everyone agreed that if they decided to add a new activity, they would eliminate an old one. The children didn't mind the new system; they don't realize they are learning to incorporate an important life skill of setting boundaries in their lives.

Brendan talks to them frequently about the need to eliminate, streamline, or delegate when schedules get too busy. He's also working to help the family schedule into their lives some time to relax together.

11. Put Your Foot Down Around Procrastinators

Do you hate it when you are meeting someone and he is always late? Or when someone on your team procrastinates and holds up the whole project you're working on? If so, you need to figure out where to set boundaries.

When you've waited for someone arriving late for a lunch

meeting, you might say, "Sorry you were tied up in traffic. I went ahead and ordered my meal because I have only an hour for lunch." Or you can stop setting up lunch meetings with that person. Depending on how much their being late bothers or stresses you, you can either tell them why you are no longer meeting with them or not.

Of course, in many work situations, you can't always stop meeting with someone, so another option would be to have the meetings at your office. It won't matter if that person is late; you can continue working. Or if possible, meet with a different individual from that company or organization.

If you can avoid an in-person meeting, try getting together by phone. If that's not possible, can you make the appointment for the end of the day so that if he arrives late, it won't disrupt your entire day or throw off other meetings?

Sometimes you cannot make changes and simply have to put up with the late arrival. In those cases, do some stress busting so this doesn't become a high-anxiety experience every time. If meetings at work often start late because key people (such as the boss) keep everyone waiting, then don't schedule another appointment immediately afterward. Who needs that kind of pressure? Set it up so that if the meeting starts late and ends late, you can still have time to make it to wherever you have to be.

Instead of fretting while you wait, you can try turning that time into a relaxing opportunity by either chatting with and getting to know your co-workers or bringing along some work you can do while you wait.

Bree used to feel nervous and resentful while waiting for a latecomer at a restaurant. Now she always brings to lunch or dinner meetings a carrying case with magazines and articles and uses it as a relaxing golden opportunity to catch up on her reading.

When the procrastinator is on your team or committee, you might try saying, "Since your procrastination is holding up the project, either you can write an e-mail to the bosses explaining that you caused the delay or I can write it. Which do you prefer?" Harsh sounding? Yes. But sometimes a procrastinator is clueless about the consequences of her actions.

Sal's committee had way too many meetings about a procrastinator sabotaging a fund-raising event, so finally the chairman spoke to the culprit. His reply was, "Sorry. I thought you guys were real laid-back about deadlines. I didn't know you were upset. I can bring things in on time from now on." Everyone on Sal's team was astonished at how easily the message was taken and how simple it was to solve the problem.

When someone's behavior is causing your stress, speak up. You seldom have the power to set boundaries on other people's behavior (although in Sal's case, a simple discussion did accomplish that) but you can set boundaries on your part of the relationship or situation.

Thoughts to Ponder

Time is the coin of your life. It is the only coin you have, and only you can determine how it will be spent. Be careful lest you let other people spend it for you.
—Carl Sandburg

Your children need your presence more than your presents.

—Jesse Jackson

You can do anything, you just can't do everything.

—Anonymous

The most desired gift of love is not diamonds or roses or chocolate. It is focused attention. Love concentrates so intently on another that you forget yourself at the moment. Attention says, "I value you enough to give you my most precious asset—my time."

—Rick Warren, *The Purpose Driven Life*

We must be willing to get rid of the life we've planned, so as to have the life that is waiting for us.

—Joseph Campbell

"Kindly let me help you or you will drown," said the monkey, putting the fish safely up in a tree.

—Alan Watts

Extra Credit

1. Do you ever let a ten-minute, fairly unimportant job take days out of your life?
2. Do you give more control of your life than you would like to technology?

3. Do you need to set boundaries on certain people in your life? Who are they and how will you do that?

_____

_____

_____

4. Do you need to set boundaries on the time you spend working? How will you do that?

_____

_____

_____

5. Do you need to set boundaries on projects? How will you do that?

_____

_____

_____

6. Do you need to set boundaries on commitments? On saying yes to requests? With whom and how will you do that?

_____

_____

_____

7. Do you have some negative expectations of experiences or situations that you need to set a boundary on or recast in a positive

way? What are the situations and what can you do to turn them around?

_____

_____

_____

_____

_____

8. Do you need to set boundaries on your schedule? How will you do that?

_____

_____

_____

9. What other areas cause stress for you? Can you set any boundaries on them? How will you do that?

_____

_____

_____

CHAPTER 7

Strive to Recharge Your Battery Daily

AT A MEETING, BOB RAN INTO HIS friend Ken, who is head of human resources for a large corporation. Ken was talking about how he was given this year's United Way campaign to run and all his many planned activities to try to generate 100 percent participation. Bob said, "Holy cow, Ken, you better watch out or you'll burn out."

Ken replied, "Naw, that'll never happen." When Bob asked how he could be so sure, Ken told him, "Every night after dinner, I go for a brisk invigorating walk with the kids, and if that doesn't shake off the stress of the day, I sit down and bang away at the piano. That works for me every time."

Later that evening, Bob was filling in his wife on how Ken was doing, and he said, "The thing that surprises me the most is that he has a *plan* for sidestepping burnout, you know, for recharging his battery if he gets stressed out. Who ever does that?"

His wife replied, "Lots of people, including me. Didn't you ever notice that if I have a rotten day at work, I come home and do yoga, and end the evening by taking a warm bath? And that nurtures my spirit and my mind, and my body."

You might think that in your life there are days when the work and responsibilities keep popping up, the time flies by, and at day's end, there is no time or energy left for activities to revitalize yourself. So you think that's just the way your life is. But it doesn't have to be.

Many people who have high-stress jobs, extreme deadlines, or overwhelming responsibilities manage to stay healthy, calm, and serene because they know how to manage stress. Randy Davis, founder of the Strategic Millionaire, says his best way to recharge is to avoid becoming overwhelmed. "I stay crystal clear on my purpose and passion. I always ask, 'What is the outcome of this activity?' I've become ruthlessly brutal in prioritizing. I might have a hundred things coming at me but only ten are truly important. That's what I focus on."

It's a fun exercise to ask people what they do to relieve stress. Some people have to think long and hard about it; others know exactly what their plan is. You often learn new information about friends you have known for years. People say things like, "I've worked with Joe for ages and never knew he played bagpipes," or "Bea has lived next door since last summer and I just discovered she has a passion for Lithuanian weaving."

Ten Tips for Reinvigorating Yourself and Reducing Stress

Sometimes the battery recharger is a passion; sometimes it's a simple ritual or technique. Even people who seem to have no opportunity to recharge have figured out little luxuries that mean the world to them. Here are some popular, effective tips on how to replenish yourself, especially during times of stress.

1. DUST OFF YOUR GREEN THUMB

Whether you putter around in a garden, maintain houseplants, or nurture a windowsill herb garden, working with plants can be very relaxing. Cheryl is a wife and mother of four sons, one of whom is a fifteen-year-old with autism and attention deficit/hyperactivity disorder. She wrote, "I sleep well only when he's down for the night and the family is there to help if he decided to get up during the night. I cannot allow myself to sleep when Lance is awake unless his personal care attendant or family members are there to watch him.

"Yes. I do recharge my battery. I *have* to! Planting amaryllis and poinsettias are my great stress busters."

2. TAKE CHARGE OF TAKING CARE OF YOU

In my keynotes and training sessions, when I ask audiences, "Who takes care of you?" they give a vast variety of replies. People say that their spouses take care of them or their parents, kids, families, or friends.

Some believe that their employer or organization or the government (oh, really?) will take care of them. Some seem to think that life in general or some vague entity out there will be their caretaker or that simply because they do all the right things, someone somewhere will care for them. Several people tell me that God takes care of them and I, too, believe that God cares for us, but I also believe that the Lord helps those who help themselves.

There's the old joke about a fellow who prayed to God to win the lottery . . . and didn't win. The next week he was on his knees again praying to win. Again, no luck. The third week he prayed with all his heart to win the lottery, and again didn't win. At this point, he was so angry that he yelled at God, "I've prayed so hard to win the lottery. Why haven't you helped me?" And he heard a booming voice answer, "Meet me halfway. Buy a ticket!"

You've got to do your part. If you're stressed, learn stress management techniques. If you're depressed, find a therapist who is a good match for you. With a little creativity, you can find forms of self-care in the most trying of situations. Even road warriors who travel constantly can create systems to care for themselves.

Linda Brakeall, author, speaker, and self-proclaimed general hell-raiser, e-mailed me her self-care strategy: "Travel is my biggest stress, so here are my 'on the road' stress busters. I force myself to get extra sleep, I carry my own pillow and comfort items like essential oils (lavender is good as a soothing agent!), I take a shower as soon as I get to my hotel room and wash off the travel vibes. Really makes a difference.

"I take trashy novels and other fiction with me as a treat because I read only work-related nonfiction at home, and call in every night to talk with my honey. I eat a high-protein, low carb, no-sugar diet when traveling and *no* liquor.

"Every day I try to take a walk to absorb more oxygen, which is energizing, and I bring extra vitamin B, E, & C with me."

Once, when I asked the question "Who takes care of you?" a

woman replied, "I do, but I'm not doing a very good job." Don't leave it up to someone else—you are in charge of taking care of you.

3. ASK FOR WHAT YOU NEED

Don't expect others to know what you need. They don't have a crystal ball.

Ummi and her children laugh about the time she was fed up and told her family, "Stay away from me. Keep out of my face. I need space." Then the very next day, she had a fender bender, and when she came home, she very pathetically said with a sigh, "I'm so upset. I wish someone would just give me a hug."

Sometimes you need space; sometimes you need an embrace. Needs change all the time.

Ellen, a nurse, recently explained to me that in Germany, when you want to celebrate a special birthday, *you* throw the party. That way, you have the type of party you want, as well as the people you would like to have there with you.

Have you ever had someone ask you, "What do you want for your birthday?" What do you say? Did you ever say "nothing" and feel disappointed when that's exactly what you got?

Don't sit around waiting and hoping for someone to come along, read your mind, and handle your stress. If you know what you need from family and friends to bolster your efforts at reducing stress, ask for what you want.

4. ADD MORE FUN TO YOUR LIFE

Georgia went on a quest to find ways to eliminate her stress. Her minister told her that would be like taking a bucket full of water out of a lake. The "hole" will simply fill in. If you could wave a magic wand to make all your stress go away, it would be replaced with new stress. And sometimes the new demands on you are ten times worse than the ones you had before.

The secret is that in the midst of demands being made upon you, you have to find ways of adding joy and fun to your life. You must discover what you love and make time for it.

BUT WHAT IF I DON'T KNOW HOW TO HAVE FUN?

- What did you love to do as a kid? Ride a bike? Finger-paint? Whistle? Jump rope double Dutch? Do it!
- Learn one new great joke and tell it all month long.
- Sing or play an instrument you loved as a child. If you can't find someone to join you, start off singing, dancing, or playing music by yourself or with your children. If you are too shy to do karaoke in public, ask for your own karaoke machine or see if a friend might own one and let you "play." You might even consider taking music lessons or an acting class at a local college.
- If there's a live concert of your favorite music anywhere in your area, or a sports event (not at all the same as watching it on TV), make time to attend. If you wait until you get the time, it'll never happen. You need to nurture your spirit now.

- What is something you've always wanted to do?
- Cook a meal where the making of the meal is fun for the whole family (put a pizza together, chop stuff for tacos, create your own rollups).
- Try some time spent outdoors in the fresh air, even if you think you're not an "outdoor person." Walk around your block or through a park or botanical garden. Plant a few flowers or tomato plants. Try this alone or with someone. You never know what you might discover.
- Get back to playing with kids. None of your own? Volunteer to work with an organization that lets you spend time with kids. They will teach you a lesson about fun.
- If you have children, schedule time with them separate from working on homework or pushing them to do chores. Just have time to play or talk or walk together.

5. PRACTICE MEDITATION

Rosita attended my seminar and said, "I used to think meditation was just sitting and not thinking, and I couldn't do that. But I believe meditation is any time you really focus on something.

"Setting a beautiful table, even if dinner is only for yourself, can be a soothing, focused meditation. Walking or knitting or working on a hobby or listening to my favorite music—or dancing to it—can be a soothing, focused meditation.

"I multitask sometimes, but when I need to get balanced, to get centered, then I just purely focus on doing one thing, and doing it well, doing it beautifully. That's my soothing meditation."

The group was spellbound listening to Rosita.

Then Paul spoke up. "I find that walking is my meditation. I used to walk listening to CDs but now I just listen to the sounds of life and pay attention to my breathing. If thoughts come to me, I give them a bit of attention, then send them on their way and go back to paying attention to my walking or breathing.

"I used to feel guilty leaving the house and going for a walk when there's so much to do, but now I know that walk will leave me clearer thinking and energized."

Cody, a CFO, said, "My way of meditating is I keep a gratitude journal. Every day I write down three things I'm grateful for. My attitude has changed, and I don't react with extreme stress like I used to."

6. TAKE REFRESHING BREAKS

Rick, a physical therapy technician, told me, "When things start to pile up on me, I build a break time into my schedule. Maybe a two-hour lunch or sleep an extra hour or two, or work hard for a couple of days so I can take time off to watch a ball game—guilt free."

Alison, a certified public accountant in public practice, described her "recharge" break to me: "I play with my daughter who is almost two. I don't worry about the clients, laundry, dishes, filing, or paperwork because none of that matters to her! She's the 'little thing' that reminds me of why I work hard."

Here's a step-by-step recipe for a refresher break from a single mother of five: "I have cookies and tea while I read something (the newspaper or a novel) to take me mentally away from the tasks that are depressing or overwhelming. I give myself an hour and always put two or three cookies on a plate so I don't eat the whole box."

7. MAKE AN APPOINTMENT WITH YOURSELF

If you're like many people, you need and want to make time for what is of value to you, but at the end of the day—after pushing to be productive and effective—there just is never any time or energy left for those other important life factors, so you say, "Maybe tomorrow." But when you have zero time for those most important things in life, that's when you most need to step off that hamster wheel and do something to recharge your battery.

Make an appointment with yourself to do something you enjoy—and be as vigilant in honoring that commitment as you would if the appointment was with someone important. After all, it is.

Have you ever heard someone say, "Wow! I've been so busy today; I haven't even had time to go to the bathroom." Now I ask you, who do they think is in charge of taking care of *that*?

If you would just make the time to stop, take a break, go for a walk, or take a nap (or—for heaven's sake—go to the bathroom, if need be), you would most likely return to your job feeling energized and much more productive and effective.

Mike Dooley, an author and professional speaker, sends out a daily e-mail signed from "the Universe." One that addressed time said:

> There's so much time in a day, you could have breakfast, lunch and dinner on 3 different continents. You could outline the book you're going to write, start the screenplay adaptation, and watch "Gone With the Wind," before the sun even sets. Spend a day at work, and still have 16 hours

left over. Or you could just think 10,000 different thoughts as you tool all over. Hey, the record for climbing Mt. Everest is under 9 hours, leaving 15 to nap and go Yeti searching.

There's so much time in a day. So much. Especially when one stops claiming there's so little of it, huh?

You're rich,
The Universe

BUT I'LL HAVE TO CATCH UP ON SO MUCH WORK LATER

Do you worry that if you take some time to nurture yourself that you'll have to work like a dog to catch up on all the work you ignored? Maybe once in a while that will happen, but if you are feeling refreshed and re-created, you'll probably find that you can get that work done much quicker than when you were just plodding along, going from one task to another with no enthusiasm.

To cut down on the number of e-mails waiting for you, set your e-mail to send an automatic reply that says how long you will be away from the office. If possible, arrange for a colleague to be willing to be contacted in case of emergency. You could program a similar outgoing message for your voice mail system, saying when you will return and offering an alternate number for someone covering emergencies. When you do return to work, look at e-mail from the most important people first. Consider saving low-priority e-mail in a folder to be read later.

Shannon told of pushing herself from project to project, never taking a break because she was determined to prevent a work pileup. Then she caught the worst cold she's ever had and was so sick she could hardly get out of bed. She missed four days of work, and when she returned, there were stacks of paper to work on all over her desk. But she realized that she wasn't buried by that crush of work. Now she takes "recharge breaks" by planning her breaks and getting a lot of things done before she leaves so she doesn't have to play catch-up when she returns to work.

8. Banish Guilt

If your doctor told you, "You must exercise a certain number of times per week," would you question whether you deserve to spend that much time and energy on yourself? Of course not. Yet how many people say they want to exercise but can't find the time? They usually find the time and energy to take care of others, but not themselves. They may feel they are being selfish if they go to the gym when they could be spending more time with their mate, children, or friends. That's what you focus on when the guilt strikes. You need to tell yourself—and to believe—that you deserve to do what's needed to recharge your battery. Then you'll see that guilt start to evaporate.

Patricia said, "If I did something just for me, I couldn't live with myself. I would feel so selfish and everyone would wonder how I could pamper myself like that."

Do you find yourself nodding in agreement? What's the solution?

If by "did something just for me" you mean all day every day, that's not what I'm advocating. Yes, you might know a few people who disguise their selfishness as self-care, but they are not many and they are not you. By taking just a small amount of time regularly to do something that re-creates your spirit and refreshes your soul, you will find yourself feeling more energized and able to continue the good work that you do.

9. Boost Your Energy Level

There is no denying that during especially busy periods you are so exhausted you're ready to keel over, and you can't imagine doing anything other than falling into bed. But sometimes fatigue and lack of desire to do things you normally enjoy are signs of burnout.

Dr. Norman Vincent Peale often said, "Enthusiasm creates energy." Everyone has different ways of generating enthusiasm. For some, it's reconnecting with old friends or spending time with grandchildren. For others it's a hobby or some form of artistic expression. Have you ever experienced being so enthusiastic about a project or hobby that you wind up working on it way past your usual bedtime, but the next day you feel just fine? The energy is there.

Each of us has to discover for ourselves what we will be enthusiastic about. The search is worth the effort because the energy created by enthusiasm gives us back our zest for living.

TWELVE ENERGY BOOSTERS

1. Exercise. Just thirty minutes of walking three or four times a week will dramatically increase your energy. The exercise might tire you out at first, but in a short time you'll feel your fatigue melt away.

2. Decrease your intake of caffeine and sugar. Their energy bursts are only temporary. The crash they cause afterward will leave you more tired than before.

3. Increase your intake of fruits and veggies. This—combined with number two—will not only add to your energy but might put you in a better mood.

4. Get enough sleep. The amount needed varies from person to person, so it's up to you to figure out your optimum hours of sleep. Not too much, but enough to leave you refreshed.

5. Consider "power naps" (if possible). They can either revive you or leave you feeling more exhausted. Like the ideal amount of sleep you need, this is something only you can figure out.

6. Drink plenty of water. Dehydration can make you feel slow and sluggish. If you drink any caffeinated beverages (coffee, tea, or soda) you will be more dehydrated, so make certain to drink plenty of water afterward.

7. Do something that's fun.

8. Take breaks. Any break can energize you—a five-minute midmorning break stepping outside and breathing fresh air; eating lunch away from your desk; setting aside a

weekend day as a re-creation day free of work; or a two-week trip.

9. Eat a midmorning or midafternoon energizer. Instead of sugar or caffeine, try a handful of nuts (providing protein and omega-3) or an apple with low-fat yogurt or low-fat cheese.

10. Get fresh air. Whether it's stepping outside for a few minutes or a two-mile walk, you will find fresh air clears your head and perks you up without fail.

11. Consider learning some yoga. The deep breathing, stretching, and twisting soothe tired muscles, increase oxygen intake, improve circulation, and aid digestion, all of which will help you feel energized and give you a sense of well-being.

12. Eat a variety of foods. To eat only one certain kind of food will prevent your getting the amount of vitamins and minerals you need for optimum health. For example, a diet of mostly carbohydrates tends to lack potassium and magnesium, which are energy boosters.

Herman told me he didn't quite understand the idea that enthusiasm creates energy until one particularly difficult work day. He came home feeling burned out and exhausted, and announced to his family, "I'm going to be in a state of total collapse tonight. Don't expect me to do anything, I'm going to be a horizontal vegetable. A couch potato. Got it?"

Five minutes later, the phone rang. It was one of his close friends who had moved to the other end of the country. "Hi, Herman, it's Rudy. Guess what. I'm in town for a conference. Can you get away tonight to meet for a drink?"

Herman was astonished to find that his exhaustion was gone. Totally. He was up and dressed and out the door in minutes, and he had a great visit with his friend.

10. GET MORE—AND BETTER—SLEEP

Sometimes you might be fatigued because you aren't getting enough rest when you go to sleep. This can affect your health and your stress level—even how long you live—much more than you think. If you have trouble sleeping, take a look at the tips below to help you rest better at night. Then combine them with a few of the energy-boosting tips, and you may find your fatigue melting away in spite of your overscheduled life.

FIFTEEN STEPS TO A GOOD NIGHT'S SLEEP

1. Make your bedroom a restful place. Clear out clutter, try scented candles, incorporate your favorite beautiful things—pictures, pillows, attractive sheets, flowers, wonderful decorations. Make it a welcoming, soothing sanctuary.

2. Protect your bedroom from office work, watching television, or playing video games (unless it helps you fall asleep).

3. When it's time to sleep, make the bedroom dark, cool, and quiet.

4. Avoid heavy eating before bedtime. If you must snack, stick to peanut butter, turkey, bananas, or other foods rich in tryptophan, which has a natural calming effect.

5. Try sipping warm milk or herbal tea to help you doze off. Remember when mothers used to give kids warm milk before bedtime? It still works.

6. For at least three to six hours before bedtime, no caffeine, nicotine, or alcohol. Some people need to put strict limits on caffeine, such as mornings only or none after two P.M. Pay attention to what your body tells you.

7. Exercise helps you sleep, but not close to (within three hours of) bedtime.

8. Nap no later than midafternoon, and not so long that it interferes with your sleep. Pay attention to how naps affect you to help you determine how long a nap you need to feel refreshed but not wide awake at bedtime.

9. Keep a regular sleep/wake schedule. Go to bed and wake up within two hours of the same time every day, even on your days off.

10. Consider wearing socks to bed. Could it be cold feet that are keeping you awake?

11. Keep a pen and pad of paper nearby to write down your worries or things to do, so you can free up your mind to drift off to dreamland.

12. Put work aside at least two to three hours before bedtime and switch to something that relaxes you.

13. If you are still tossing and turning twenty minutes after going to bed, get up and read, listen to soothing music,

or do something else relaxing for a while. Don't fight sleeplessness.

14. Let light help you. Dim the light for a few hours before you go to bed and light up the room or go out into sunshine soon after you wake up to help set your brain's internal clock to your sleeping and waking schedule.

15. If you continue to struggle with going to sleep, consider a visit to a sleep specialist.

Vince bounces out of bed early during the week, so he used to sleep until noon on the weekend "to catch up on sleep." But when he slept that late, he usually felt heavy and sluggish for the rest of the day. He often heard that it's important to keep a consistent wake-up schedule, but he didn't think it applied to him.

One Saturday he had to work, so he woke up at his usual workday time. He was surprised to notice that he felt great all day and even more surprised that he seemed to have more energy that Monday and the rest of the week. Vince now tries to wake up around the same time even on weekends because he is convinced this new schedule has helped to improve his general energy level.

THOUGHTS TO PONDER

Without enthusiasm you are doomed to a life of mediocrity but with it you can accomplish miracles.

—OG MANDINO

Long ago when men cursed and beat the ground with sticks, it was called witchcraft . . . Today, it's called golf.

—ANONYMOUS

People are lonely who build walls instead of bridges.

—MARTIN BUBER

When you love what you do and you believe that it matters, what could be more fun?

—MARTHA GRAHAM

Sometimes our light almost goes out but is blown again into flames by an encounter with another human being. Each of us owes the deepest thanks to those who have rekindled this inner light.

—ALBERT SCHWEITZER

Those who bring sunshine to the lives of others cannot keep it from themselves.

—JAMES M. BARRIE

Don't ask yourself what the world needs, ask yourself what makes you come alive. And then go do that. Because what the world needs are people who have come alive.

—HAROLD WHITMAN

Be gentle with yourself.

—MAX EHRMANN

He who cannot rest cannot work; he who cannot let go cannot hold on.

—HARRY EMERSON FOSDICK

EXTRA CREDIT

1. If you were given twenty-four hours with no agenda or responsibilities, what would you do?

   _____

2. If you were given seven days with no agenda or responsibilities, what would you do?

   _____

   _____

3. If you could wave a magic wand and have the time, money, and talent to do whatever you want to do, what would it be?

   _____

   _____

   _____

4. What makes you laugh or feel happy?

   _____

   _____

5. What are you enthusiastic about? Passionate about?

_____

_____

6. What were you doing the last time you felt relaxed? Joyful? Re-created?

_____

_____

7. Decide on one thing to recharge your battery that you enjoy or adds fun to your life, or something you are enthusiastic or passionate about. What re-creates you?

_____

_____

8. Schedule some time this week for yourself (even if it's only twenty minutes). If you still struggle with reasons why you procrastinate about recharging your battery, list those reasons here.

_____

_____

_____

_____

CHAPTER 8

Now Let's Put It All Together

GERRI HOPED TO MAIL THANK-YOU NOTES two weeks after her wedding, but when two months had gone by, she felt that the little short note cards she had purchased were no longer adequate. At that point, she felt she owed people more than one or two sentences on a thank-you note.

Every time she thought about writing those notes, she felt her heart speeding up and she would become so stressed out that she'd end up with a blazing headache. She was overwhelmed at the thought of writing thank-you notes to 350 people. She wouldn't ask her new husband for help because she had promised him ten days after the wedding that she'd take care of it, and she hated to admit to him that she hadn't done them.

Then a third month went by, so she felt she owed everyone a letter, maybe with some made-up excuses telling everyone why she was so late thanking them. Her husband's mother had already commented that relatives hadn't received thank-yous yet. Gerri's husband offered to help but still nothing was done. She could not get herself to do this dreaded job, and she was starting to feel sick about it.

You've probably seen something like this—maybe even lived it—a hundred times. A bit of stress hits you, so you put off a few things. Then one of the tasks you procrastinated about escalates, causing you even greater stress.

You started reading this book probably because you were feeling overworked, overscheduled, or overwhelmed. Maybe you wanted to learn more about time management without adding to your stress. Or maybe you wanted to ease your stress without diluting your productivity, effectiveness, or efficiency. This book has provided strategies, techniques, tips, and ideas for melting away your stress and stress-related symptoms. But none of them will help you if you put off implementing them. Here are five simple steps to help catapult you into action.

1. PUT THE SITUATION INTO PERSPECTIVE

Sharon, who works at the counter in the post office, misplaced the forms for money orders. Her customer was kept waiting while she searched for and finally found them. As she completed his order, she repeatedly apologized for keeping him waiting. Then, with a warm smile, he calmly said, "If this is the worst mistake you make today, you are having a great day."

Sharon said that has become her motto when she needs to change her reaction. When she was in a panic because she thought she'd lost her purse, she said to herself, "Well, if this is the worst thing that ever happens to me then I'm having a pretty good life." She repeats that phrase when she's frantic because a long train is causing her to be late for an appointment, when she's upset that her teenage son got a speeding ticket, when she's disappointed because she didn't get a promotion.

When she was feeling betrayed by a co-worker, she snapped herself out of it by repeating, "Well, if this is the worst thing a friend ever does to me, I guess I'll survive." She says that odd little phrase has helped her gain perspective and shake off stress in dozens of potentially stress-causing situations.

SELF-TALK THAT ENABLES YOU TO CHANGE YOUR REACTION OR RESPONSE

If this is the worst thing that ever happens to me, then I'm leading a pretty good life.

If this is the worst mistake I ever make, then I'm leading a pretty good life.

If this is the worst thing my child ever does, then I'm leading a pretty good life.

If this goes wrong, I'll survive it.

It doesn't make sense to expect perfection from myself, others, or life. This is an imperfect world.

Everyone doesn't have to do what I want them to do or do things my way, and I'm OK with that.

It's OK for me to not agree with someone or to tell someone I'm hurt.

It's OK for me to be too tired or busy to do something that is not important to me.

Will this matter six months from now?

Will I still be worried about this a year from now?

Worry is unproductive. I'll write down my worry in a worry notebook, date it, and stop dwelling on it.

I don't have to solve everyone's problems.

No matter what is going wrong in my life, I will look for something to be grateful for today.

Instead of blaming someone for this, it's OK for me to take responsibility for it.

Taking responsibility for something doesn't mean I will blame myself constantly for everything wrong with the world or my life.

My anger doesn't hurt the one I'm angry with but it can make me sick.

It's OK if others don't do something to make me happy. I'm in charge of becoming happy.

Why am I upset? No, really, what specifically is upsetting me? What part of this is upsetting me?

So what if they didn't like it? I like it.

I made a mistake; now what can I learn from it?

So what if they don't agree? I have a right to have an opinion.

It's OK for me to ask for help and it's OK for someone to re-fuse me.

It's not possible to make everyone happy.

There's always someone who will dislike/hate/criticize me.

2. Decide What You're Going to Do

One of the biggest causes of procrastination is difficulty making a decision.

Brad, a Realtor, has dreamed of starting his own small restaurant since college. He desperately wants to leave the stressful life of real estate, and even though he knows he will have to work hard running a restaurant, he feels that doing what he loves will omit much of the stress involved. He knows what he needs to do but he hasn't even decided what steps to take. Brad says his life has been so busy he doesn't have time, but the reality is that he hasn't made a clear decision to do anything about it.

Karen has planned on starting an exercise program as a way to prevent burnout and also says that she hasn't had time to do anything about it. The reality is, she just hasn't decided to take some steps to get started.

Abbey is embarrassed by all the clutter in her house, and just looking at the piles of paper and stuff leaves her feeling exhausted. Once she misplaced an electric bill and another time she lost a wedding invitation and missed the wedding. She has been planning to declutter her house for months, and she's aware that just as her clutter took a long time to accumulate, it won't disappear in a day. But she can't decide what to tackle first.

Regardless of what's causing you stress, decide what your first step will be in relieving it or working toward your goal. It can be something simple. But commit to doing something—give yourself a timetable for when you will finish doing whatever it is.

Andrew was in his forties, overworked, and stressed out. He liked his job but felt unfulfilled. Since high school he had been aware that he had a gift for writing but was too tired or unmoti-vated to write on his own at night or on the weekend. Aware that doing something he was enthusiastic about would reenergize him, he decided that during the fall he would enroll in a ten-week con-tinuing education writing class at his local community college, even though he felt he didn't have one spare moment in his busy life.

He loved the class and was especially inspired by a class assign-ment to "write about something you know." Andrew was an avid gardener and his article combined spirituality and gardening. The teacher said, "Andrew, I think you have the beginning of an excel-lent book here." And so, Andrew is now working on his first book.

3. START SMALL

Yes, you may have a gazillion stress-busting things you want to do—don't start with the biggest, most challenging thing. One small change is a great way to start.

Instead of committing to exercising every day of your life till the day you die, start with a ten- or fifteen-minute walk during your lunch hour or after work. Rather than trying to change your whole personality, just put up a few reminders that striving for excellence is achievable and perfection usually isn't.

Gerri, the bride at the beginning of the chapter, was totally overwhelmed at the thought of writing 350 thank-you letters. First of all, she needed to realize that many people came as cou-ples, so she'd really be writing 175 to 200 thank-yous. But that is still overwhelming, so her best bet was to develop a time-saving system. She designated a spot where she gathered up all she needed into one place—the stationery, envelopes, stamps, address book, everything—and then was able to leave it all together in that spot for several weeks. She also cut back on her expectations— instead of writing letters offering lengthy excuses, she wrote notes that focused on the couple's gratitude.

She decided on a realistic and attainable goal of writing to five or ten people each evening. If she watched TV, she wrote notes or addressed envelopes during commercials. Once she did this for several evenings, she realized it wasn't the whole job that she dreaded, it was just getting started. She decided she could proba- bly start doing more thank-yous each evening. And eventually, that job was done.

4. Use a Timer

When Andrew decided to take a writing class one night a week he found that the more he enjoyed it, the easier it was to make time for the class each week. I can hear you starting to panic. Fear not. Nobody is expecting you to give up any huge amount of time.

It's your stress. It's your time. It's your life.

The fact is, most people can carve out one hour occasionally. Not an hour every day, but almost everyone can free up one hour per week. That's where you start.

Identify what change you want to make in order to take control of the stress in your life, and give it one hour per week. It might be an hour of work streamlining your files so it's easier for you to retrieve information, or it might be one hour of an activity that recharges you, such as reading, working on a hobby, or meditat- ing. Set a kitchen timer for sixty minutes.

Bill, a purchasing agent, used to say that he could time everything in his head, and he could. But then he realized that the tick-tick-tick of a timer really adds a sense of urgency to the job. Now he keeps a kitchen timer shaped like an apple on his desk and uses it every day—to remind him of a conference call, to place time limits on chatty vendor calls when he wants to set boundaries on those conversations, and of course for his one-hour blitz of his goals. He can't remember how he was able to stay organized before he kept a timer on his desk.

During that hour of working on your goal, there are only two rules:

1. Ignore everything else. Not forever, just while the timer is ticking. This includes phone calls. (If you weren't there or if your phone was turned off, they would have to leave a voice mail. They can survive doing that while the timer is ticking.)
2. No breaks. If you forgot to get a glass of water, cup of coffee, or that mint mocha frappuccino before you started, you have to wait until the timer dings.

It's the interruptions and the breaks that sabotage our lives. How often have you started off with a firm commitment to go through your old e-mails, file what's important, and delete the rest, but you keep stopping to check your incoming messages. Then you decide to take just one little minute to make two quick phone calls and follow up on requests or questions raised in the phone calls. Suddenly you look at the clock and you decide, "Well, it's too late to get started on organizing my e-mail today. I'll have to tackle that when I get the time."

Or you look around and see that you have started fifteen tasks and completed none of them. You say, "Well, I was multitasking." You might be astonished at how much work you accomplish in one hour when you follow those two rules of no interruptions and no breaks.

5. It's Time to Do the Worst First and Reward Yourself

Bob's job included writing up a report every Monday morning logging the phone calls received over the weekend on the emergency line of the mental health center where he worked. The report was to be sent to the human resources department and took only about twenty minutes to write. But often that report still was not completed in the afternoon.

It was as if a black cloud of dread hung over Bob's head all day long. If someone asked him to go out to lunch with them, Bob would say he couldn't go because he still had that danged report to do. He knew if he could get himself to do that report first, he would feel free the rest of the day, but he just couldn't get himself going on it. Then he heard about using rewards to motivate himself.

He really loved coffee. So his plan was to allow himself one cup at home on Monday. Then once he was at work, no coffee until the report was complete. Now every Monday, Bob starts work at nine A.M. and has that report to HR by nine thirty. Then he makes a big deal out of "going down the hall to meet with Juan Valdez and his burro for my cup of fresh roasted mountain-grown coffee."

Nothing worked to get him to do this report first thing in the morning until he came up with this coffee-reward idea. Two years later, Bob still turns in his report by nine thirty, then races down the hall for his beloved cup of fresh roasted mountain-grown coffee. He says, "If it works, don't fix it."

When you find the right reward, it will help you reach many goals. Just don't kid yourself and say, "Well, the accomplishment of the job itself is enough reward for me." Heck, if that's true, why did you put it off in the first place?

Jocelyn found herself working overtime almost every evening and usually brought home work, which took up most of her Saturday. Most of Sunday was spent doing laundry, cleaning the house, and grocery shopping, so there was never time to re-create herself.

Jocelyn would return to work on Monday feeling tired and dragging from all she did the previous week and weekend. Then, instead of working at 100 percent, she often performed much of her work at 50 to 70 percent. As a result, she didn't complete what was expected of her, so she ended up putting in hours of overtime.

She knew she needed a change and decided to do some journaling to try to clarify her thoughts and values. Immediately she recognized that what she hated most about all her overtime was missing time with her children. She loved doing activities with them like going to the zoo, museums, the beach, and the movies, and she hadn't done any of that in almost a year. A chill gripped her heart as she thought about how fast her children were growing up and what she was missing with them.

Jocelyn decided that in the coming week she would write out what she needed to accomplish each day. Then she would keep focused on those goals and push to work at top speed to get everything complete. She set boundaries that she would not work past five thirty and was not going to work more than one hour on any work she brought home. She was excited about her plan and enthusiastic about her intended reward: a day with the kids at the zoo.

Jocelyn's enthusiasm enabled her to feel more energized and she completed everything she planned for that week. On Saturday, she told her sons about her plan, how she wrote out her goals and reached all of them. And now she was rewarding herself with a trip to the zoo, and they were all invited to join her. The whoops and hollers showed Jocelyn the joy the boys felt, and she felt it too. What a magnificent lesson to teach them. Reach for goals, work hard, and then give yourself a fun reward.

Having a balance between work and play is very important. According to Neil Fiore, author of *The Now Habit: A Strategic Program for Overcoming Procrastination and Enjoying Guilt-Free Play*, recharging your battery and relaxing can make the difference between being productive and finishing a project or just taking forever and procrastinating. Dr. Fiore led a research project several years ago where he compared Ph.D. students who took less than two years to complete their doctoral program to those who took between three and nineteen years. The difference between those who took a short time and those who took longer had nothing to do with intellect or emotion; it was "who suffered more."

Students who took the longest had put their lives on hold; they didn't make time to enjoy themselves. They felt guilty when they were having fun because they felt as if they had a cloud of dread hanging over their heads reminding them they ought to be working. Yet when they did focus on their dissertations, they worked halfheartedly because they were so deprived of pleasure. They had created lives that were joyless. Everything took a longer time to accomplish and there was a tremendous amount of resentment.

People who completed dissertations in two years or less didn't have the same philosophy of life. They didn't set themselves up to be martyrs. They worked hard but in short bursts, dividing time between work and play or relaxation, and enjoyed their lives.

Cherish Today

By understanding stress and clarifying your values, eliminating and streamlining wherever you can, trashing perfectionism but reaching for realistic goals, setting boundaries, and recharging your battery, you can make radical, healthy changes in your life. By making just a few changes suggested in this book, you can live the life you want. You can lead a full, rich, productive life without the stress and anxiety that many people accept as part of that lifestyle.

As John Greenleaf Whittier wrote:

> *The saddest words of tongue or pen*
> *Are these four words: "It might have been."*

You will never get today back. If you have $1,000 saved and you decide to spend it on something important, you can earn another $1,000 someday and replace the amount you spent. Time is different. You will never have this day again. You cannot replace it because nothing will ever be this way again. Children in your life will never be this age again—for that matter, neither will your family or friends. Most important, *you* will never be this age again.

Maria, a cheerful, positive-thinking housecleaner, said that she moped around for weeks when she turned sixty. She now looks back on that time and believes she actually went into a depression over that birthday. When asked what pulled her out of it, she said it was her eighty-six-year-old father-in-law. He said, "Listen, Maria, no matter what age you are, there are people somewhere wishing they could be that young again." Then he grinned and said, "Me, for instance. I envy you. I wish I could be sixty again."

Maria said hearing those few words snapped her out of her deep blue funk. A few weeks later, she had a great laugh when she heard a 106-year-old woman being interviewed on TV. The woman said, "I'm doing fine, but I'm not as spry as those ninety-nine-year-old chicks."

Learn to cherish each day for what it is—not something to regret because it is flying by too fast, not a chunk of time in which to rush around trying to accomplish a gazillion tasks, but a magic twenty-four hours to be treasured on the journey of living life to the fullest and loving every minute of it.

If you have clarified your values, stopped shooting for perfection, set realistic goals, tried to eliminate and streamline every place you can, set boundaries, and figured out ways to recharge your battery daily, and none of that works because you still are working every single minute of every single day, then I presume you simply cannot make changes at this point. Even people who have high-pressure careers or are building their own business can make some small changes. For example, leaving work an hour earlier once a month to spend time with a loved one or to get a relaxing massage may be doable, though it may mean you cannot cut back on overtime the rest of the month. Or if you are caring for a very sick or difficult person, you can contact your local family service center or health department to see if any respite services might be available to you.

Making changes in your life can be extremely difficult, but it is not impossible.

My hope is that as you start this journey, you will rediscover and awaken that childlike part of you that you were born with—that part of you that loves life, that person within you who is interested and curious and excited and enthusiastic.

The actress Diane Keaton was asked in an interview, "Given what you know from your own particular life, what would you pass on to your young daughter at this moment?" Her answer was passionate. "It would be great if she had a huge, huge, huge appetite for life. I really wish that for her. I hope that she embraces it enormously—every aspect of it. Headstrong. I hope that she is strong and curious and excited and interested, because that will pull her through."

Your Personal Action Plan

It is very human to come to the end of a book and have the greatest of intentions. All kinds of resolutions are bouncing around in your brain and heart that when accomplished will make your life so much more wonderful. Then you set the book down and the phone is ringing, e-mails are pouring in, the fax machine is spewing out papers, people are pulling at you from every direction, the world is spinning faster than it used to, and every once in a while, you have fond memories of that book but cannot remember anything you wanted to do as a result of reading it. What to do?

First of all, writing your personal action plan will enable you to remember your goals and ideas anytime you want by simply picking up this book again.

Second, there is great power in writing down goals, plans, and resolutions. Somehow, what you write seeps slowly into your subconscious and sometimes later it bubbles up and nudges you to do something even though you haven't reviewed your written plans.

Third, if you regularly refer to and review your written answers, it will help you keep on the path you have chosen to travel as you move through life.

Fourth, it's fun to look at your action plan a few years down the road (so be sure to date it) and see what changes have occurred in your thinking, your behavior, and your life. List here those values that are most important in your life right now.

_____

_____

_____

_____

_____

_____

As you clarify what is important in your life and what you want to spend your time on, you will have to decide what steps to take in order to achieve your goals. To avoid getting stressed out, think about whether you need to take a course or buy some software or any kind of equipment (gardening, fishing, workout, etc.). Do you need to search for something (a used harp, a comedy improv class, an organization looking for volunteers with your talents)? Do you need to omit something from your life in order to make room for your stress busting (a group you no longer enjoy, a hobby you no longer delight in, clutter in an area that you need to use)?

List here what steps you need to take to move closer to a joyful and serene life.

_____

_____

_____

_____

_____

Is perfection still one of the standards you strive for? What message or reminder can you write here to get you back to the reality of the imperfect world we all live in?

_____

_____

_____

_____

_____

Have you discovered that some of your goals were unrealistic?
Which ones?

_____

_____

_____

To help you think about your goals for now, try imagining what
your life would be like ten years from now.

Write the date it would be ten years from now _____

Now picture yourself answering these questions not today, but
ten years from now:

a) How old are you (ten years from now)? _____

b) Where do you live? _____

c) What are you doing to earn a living?

_____

d) Who are you with? _____

e) Where have you traveled?

_____

_____

_____

_____

_____

f) Describe your proudest moment in the last ten years.

_____

_____

g) Describe a typical Saturday.

_____

_____

_____

_____

_____

_____

_____

h) What sort of things do you own?

_____

_____

_____

_____

i) Now here's a biggie: How have you changed as a person? (Would it surprise you to know that most people include something about being more relaxed and less stressed?)

_____

_____

_____

_____

_____

Now come back to the present and name one thing you can do in the next year to bring yourself closer to each of your goals in ten years.

_____

_____

What can you do in the next week to bring yourself closer to your ideal life?

_____

_____

_____

Now write three goals here that you want to accomplish in the next two years. Consider possibilities for adventure. What do you want to be when you grow up? Your goals can be social, spiritual, physical, financial, intellectual, or emotional, or have to do with relationships, pets, your home, your work, your transportation, or where you live.

_____

_____

Have you given thought to anything in your life that you can eliminate or streamline? List them here.

_____

_____

_____

_____

Are there any expectations—of someone else or you— that you are eliminating or streamlining?

_____

_____

_____

How will your life be different with these streamlinings and eliminations?

_____

_____

_____

_____

Have you decided to set any boundaries? List them here.

_____

_____

_____

_____

List at least three things you can do to recharge your battery daily. You can list lots and lots more if you choose.

_____

_____

_____

_____

_____

_____

_____

_____

Now list one thing you will do *for sure* for yourself within the next twenty-four hours.

_____

Have you ever said, "When such-and-such happens, *then* I'll be happy" or "*then* I can manage my stress" or "*then* life will be worth living"? List here all the things you would like to happen in order for you to feel happy or relaxed or as if life is worth living.

_____

_____

_____

_____

_____

What steps can you take to make any one of these things you've listed come true? List them.

_____

_____

_____

_____

OK, that's what you *can* do. Now what are you willing to do?

_____

_____

_____

_____

_____

_____

_____

_____

When I was in high school, I fell in love with a poem called "Ode" by Arthur O'Shaughnessy. You've probably heard some of the lines. It starts off: "We are the music-makers / And we are the dreamers of dreams."

I believe every one of us touches other people's dreams in a hundred different ways. Sometimes we touch others with what we do, either professionally, through our work, or personally, through our acts of kindness and our interactions with other people. Sometimes we touch others' dreams simply by being who we are. You never know when some friend or co-worker or even a child you know might be saying, "If she can make it through that illness, or if he can survive that divorce, maybe I can find the strength to make it through this tough time in my life." Or people might be saying, "If he can achieve that, maybe I can set my goals a little higher and try for a bigger dream."

ODE
(excerpt)
BY ARTHUR O'SHAUGHNESSY

> *We are the music-makers,*
> *And we are the dreamers of dreams,*
> *Wandering by lone sea-breakers,*
> *And sitting by desolate streams;*
> *World-losers and world-forsakers,*
> *On whom the pale moon gleams:*
> *Yet we are the movers and shakers*
> *Of the world for ever, it seems.*

Who are the movers and shakers of the world? You are. And you owe it to yourself to become a stress buster so you can lead a life of meaning and purpose, happiness and joy. Enjoy the journey.

THOUGHTS TO PONDER

If you want to know your past, look into your present conditions. If you want to know your future, look into your present actions.

—ANONYMOUS TIBETAN MONK

Perhaps the most valuable result of all education is the ability to make yourself do the thing you have to do, when it ought to be done, whether you like it or not.
—THOMAS HUXLEY

You don't get to choose how you're going to die, or when. You can only decide how you're going to live. Now.
—JOAN BAEZ

Much of the stress that people feel doesn't come from having too much to do. It comes from not finishing what they started.
—DAVID ALLEN

A procrastinator's work is never done.
—ANONYMOUS

Time is always on the move, even when we are not.
—ANONYMOUS

Procrastination is the passive assassin of opportunity.
—ROY WILLIAMS

He has the deed half-done who has made a beginning.
—HORACE

We know what we are, but know not what we may be.
—WILLIAM SHAKESPEARE

The aim of life is to live, and to live means to be aware:
joyously, drunkenly, serenely, divinely aware.

—HENRY MILLER

Success is not the key to happiness. Happiness is the key
to success. If you love what you are doing, you will be
successful.

—HERMAN CAIN

Most people never run far enough on their first wind to
find out they've got a second. Give your dreams all
you've got and you'll be amazed at the energy that comes
out of you.

—WILLIAM JAMES

Hans Selye, a pioneer in the understanding of human
stress, was often asked, "What is the most stressful
condition a person can face?" His unexpected response:
"Not having something to believe in."

Index

Adams, John Quincy, 112
Adams, Phillip, 64
Allen, David, 181
Andretti, Mario, 64
Angelou, Maya, 25
*The Artist's Way: A Spiritual Path
    to Higher Creativity*
    (Cameron), 49

Baez, Joan, 181
Barrie, James M., 154
boredom, 37–40
boundaries, 115–36
    balancing work and play,
        166–68
    dealing with procrastinators
        and late-comers, 131–33
    and family traditions, 128–29

importance of, 117
learning to say no, 121–23
limiting children's activities,
    130–31
limiting interruptions, 126–28
limiting time spent on phone
    calls, 124–25
and personal action plan, 177
separating work time and
    family time, 121, 166–67
setting limits on commitments,
    118
setting reachable goals,
    125–26
and stress reduction, 115–16
workloads and, 129–30
Bradshaw, John, 81
Brakeall, Linda, 140

breaks, 144–47, 149, 164–65
Buber, Martin, 154
Burnett, Leo, 88
burnout, 9, 15, 16, 20–21, 38–40,
    137–38
busy-ness, 3–4, 7–8, 54–56. *See
    also* eliminating and
    streamlining

caffeine, 149
Cain, Herman, 182
Cameron, Julia, 49
Campbell, Joseph, 134
Cantor, Eddie, 26
caregivers, 67–70
Castaneda, Carlos, 26
Cervantes, Miguel de, 112
children's activities, 92–93,
    130–31
clutter busting, 98, 161
control freaks, 57
cortisol, 11–12
Cowie, Colin, 52

Davis, Randy, 138
dehydration, 149
diet and nutrition, 149, 150, 152
Ditka, Mike, 113
do-not-do lists, 106
Dooley, Mike, 145–46
Drucker, Peter, 55

Ehrmann, Max, 154
eliminating and streamlining,
    90–114
  clutter busting, 98
  eliminating negative aspects,
    103–5
  evaluating purchases and
    priorities, 93–95
  hiring help, 101
  identifying wants *versus* needs,
    90–93
  information and paper
    overload, 98–100
  learning to say no, 97–98
  making a do-not-do list, 106
  multitasking, 107–9
  and personal action plan, 176
  scheduling specific times for,
    102–3
  using time logs, 97
e-mail, 30, 98–100, 109, 146
Emerson, Ralph Waldo, 88, 111
Emmett's Law of Goal Setting, 72
energy levels, 148–51
enthusiasm, 148–51
excellence, 51–53
exercise, 149, 150
Extra Credit sections, 6

fairy-tale people, 59–61
family traditions, 128–29

fatigue, 148–53
fervent fixers, 57–59
fight or flight response, 11
Fiore, Neil, 167–68
fizzle factor, 58–59
footprints in the snow, 85–86
Ford, Henry, 88
Fosdick, Harry Emerson, 25, 155
Franklin, Benjamin, 87
fun, 142–43

gardening, 139
Gillies, Jerry, 110
goals, 67–89
    maintaining focus on, 74–75,
        85–86, 171
    obstacles to, 72–75
    Personal Action Plan, 170–79
    recognizing unrealistic goals,
        67–69, 125–26
    relaxation and, 78–81
    sample list of life goals, 77
    setting specific and measurable
        goals, 70–72, 162–63
    and stress reduction, 75–76
    values and, 81–85
    work ethic and, 78–80
goal stoppers, 72–75
Goethe, Johann Wolfgang von, 45
Goldberg, Natalie, 26
good ol' days, 13–14, 78–80

Graham, Martha, 154
guilt, 147–48

happily ever after, 59–61
holidays, 63, 128–29
Homecoming: Reclaiming and
    Healing Your Inner Child
    (Bradshaw), 81
Horace, 181
houseplants, 139
Huxley, Thomas, 181

"if this is the worst thing...", self-
    talk phrase, 158–59
information overload, 98–100
interruptions, 109, 164–65

Jackson, Jesse, 134
James, William, 182
Johnson, Samuel, 45
Jordan, Michael, 88

Kahon, Jamie, 11
Keaton, Diane, 170
Keller, Helen, 65
Kennedy, Rose Fitzgerald, 45
Kissinger, Henry, 87

"The Lake Isle of Innisfree"
    (Yeats), 43–44
Lamott, Anne, 64

Landon, Michael, 64
Langbridge, Frederick, 25
Lao-tzu, 110
late-comers, 131–33
life goals, 75–77

Mackay, Harvey, 111
mail, 98–100, 102
Mandino, Og, 110, 153
Margin (Swenson), 41–42, 98–99
McCourt, Malachy, 96
meditation, 143–44
Miller, Henry, 182
Morley, Christopher, 44
Mortman, Doris, 110
multifocusing, 108
multitasking, 107–9

naps, 149, 152
needs *versus* wants, 90–93
negative goals, 70–72
no, learning to say, 97–98, 121–23
nourishing people, 81–82
The Now Habit (Fiore), 167–68

"Ode" (O'Shaughnessy), 179–80
O'Shaughnessy, Arthur, 179–80

Page, Susan, 110
paper and information overload,
    98–100

Peale, Norman Vincent, 148
perfectionism, 49–66
    control freaks and fervent
        fixers, 57–59
    excellence instead of, 51–53
    expectations and, 52–54
    expecting perfection in others,
        50–51
    myth of fairy-tale people and
        happily ever after, 59–61
    and personal action plan, 172–73
    productivity *versus* busy-ness,
        54–56
    sources of unrealistic
        expectations, 63
    stress and, 56–57, 61–62
Personal Action Plan, 170–79
perspective and reducing stress,
    158–60
phone calls, 102, 109, 124–25,
    126–28
positive goals, 70–72
power naps, 149
procrastinators, 131–33
productivity, 54–56

Quindlen, Anna, 65

Rand, Ayn, 87
recharging your batteries, 33,
    137–56, 145

add fun, 142–43

ask for help to reduce stress, 141

avoiding burnout, 137–38

enthusiasm and energy levels, 148–51

gardening and houseplants, 139

guilt and, 147–48

make an appointment with yourself, 145–46

meditation, 143–44

and personal action plan, 177–79

self-care strategies, 139–41

take refresher breaks, 144

rewards, 21–23, 165–68

Roger, John, 111

Rogers, Carl, 113

Rogers, Will, 44

Roosevelt, Eleanor, 46

Rubinstein, Arthur, 46

St. Patrick and King Angus, 53–54

Sandburg, Carl, 133

Schweitzer, Albert, 45, 154

Seattle, Chief, 45

self-appreciation, 21–23

self-care, 23–24, 139–41

self-love, 33–35

self-talk, 17–18, 158–60

Selye, Hans, 12, 25, 182

Shaker hymn, 112

Shakespeare, William, 112, 181

Shinn, Florence, 46

simplification. *See* eliminating and streamlining

sleep, 149, 151–53

small changes, 162–63, 169–70

Solomon, King, 87

spiritual stress, 12

spring housecleaning, 103

Stowe, Harriet Beecher, 46

streamlining. *See* eliminating and streamlining

stress
    clutter and, 98
    consequences of, 7–8, 11–12, 15
    definition of, 11, 12
    eliminating and streamlining and, 93
    freedom from *versus* management, 16
    in the good ol' days, 13–14
    identifying stressors, 26–27
    life goals and, 75–77
    modern pressures and, 14–15
    perfectionism and, 56–57, 61–62
    recharging your batteries and, 137–38
    setting boundaries and, 115–16
    values and, 32–33

stress management. *See also*
    recharging your batteries
    cherish today, 168–70
    controlling responses to
        stressors, 12, 17–18, 159–60
    first steps, 161–62
    healthy and unhealthy coping
        strategies, 16
    Personal Action Plan, 170–79
    put the situation into
        perspective, 158–60
    reward yourself, 165–68
    start small, 162–63
    use a timer, 163–65
success, 51–53, 96
Swenson, Richard, 41–42, 98–99

television, 37
Time Logs, 97
time management, 5, 19–20,
    30–33
timers, 163–64
today, cherishing, 168–70
Tolstoy, Leo, 111
toxic people, 81–82

Upanishads, 109

vacations, 13
values, 28–48
    burnout *versus* boredom, 38–40

identifying, 31–33
    incorporating values into
        lifestyle, 36–37, 41–44
    life goals and, 81–85
    living out of sync with,
        28–30
    and personal action plan,
        171–72
    self-love and, 33–35
    simplifying life and, 95–96
    time management and, 30–31
visualization, 43–44
volunteer work, 41–42

wants *versus* needs, 90–93
Warren, Rick, 134
Watts, Alan, 134
wealth, 92
Whitman, Harold, 154
Whittier, John Greenleaf, 168
Wholey, Dennis, 26
Williamson, Marianne, 110
Williams, Roy, 181
Winfrey, Oprah, 45, 64, 87
Woman's Home Companion,
    112
Wooden, John, 46
work ethic, 78–80

Yeats, William Butler, 43–44
yoga, 150

A Note on the Author

Rita emmett leads self-improvement and productivity workshops on a variety of topics, including clutter and procrastination. She is the author of *The Clutter-Busting Handbook, The Procrastinating Child,* and *The Procrastinator's Handbook.* She has appeared on *Talk of the Town* and NBC's *Today Show* and has been featured in *Time,* the *New York Times,* the *Wall Street Journal, Family Circle,* and *Parents.*

Rita would like to hear the successful ways you find to apply her different techniques and strategies to your life. You may send your story or obtain information about other products and services offered by Rita by contacting her at:

www.RitaEmmett.com
e-mail: Remmett412@aol.com

or at

Emmett Enterprises, Inc.
2331 Eastview Drive
Des Plaines, IL 60018